GIANTS

giants

Illustrated by
Julek Heller, Carolyn Scrace
and Juan Wijngaard

Devised by David Larkin
Text by Sarah Teale

Harry N. Abrams, Inc., Publishers, New York
Peacock Press/Bantam Books
New York · London · Toronto

*We are most grateful to the publishers who have
kindly allowed us to use their material:*

B.T. Batsford Limited, London
for permission to refer to and quote from Ernest W. Marwick's book
The Folklore of Orkney and Shetland (1975).

Paul Elek Limited, London
for permission to use material from
The Secret Country
by Janet and Colin Bord.
Copyright © 1976 Janet and Colin Bord (1976).

The Folklore Society London
for permission to mention material from: –
County Folk-Lore, Vol II – North Riding of Yorkshire, York and the Ainsty,
collected and edited by Mrs Gutch (1901).
County Folk-Lore,
Printed extracts no 3 – Leicestershire and Rutland,
collected and edited by Charles James Billson, M.A. (1895).
Somerset Folklore (County Folklore – Vol VIII)
by R.L. Tongue,
edited by K.M. Briggs (1965).

Alfred A. Knopf, Inc, New York
for permission to mention some of the exploits from
Paul Bunyan
by James Stevens (1925).

Penguin Books Limited, London
for permission to reprint a passage from Lewis Thorpe's translation
of Geoffrey of Monmouth's work
The History of the Kings of Britain
(Penguin Classics, London 1966) p. 196
© Lewis Thorpe, 1966.
Reprinted by permission of Penguin Books Ltd.

The Reader's Digest Association Limited, London
for permission to mention material from their book
Folklore, Myths and Legends of Britain (1973)

Routledge & Kegan Paul Limited, London
for permission to mention the story of
the Giant of Grabbist from
Folktales of England
edited by Katherine M. Briggs and Ruth L. Tongue (1965)

Walker and Company, New York
for permission to use material from
The Secret Country
by Janet and Colin Bord.
Copyright © 1976 by Janet and Colin Bord.
Used with permission of the publisher, Walker and Company.

Color reproduction by Carlton Repro International Ltd,
a division of Sir Joseph Causton & Sons Ltd, London and Eastleigh.

INTRODUCTION

"O! It is excellent
to have a giant's strength,
but it is tyrannous
to use it like a giant."
(Measure for Measure
WILLIAM SHAKESPEARE)

Strength has always been recognized as a prerequisite for survival and holders of great power, whether physical or supernatural, are traditionally both revered and reviled. National heroes in antiquity were popularly endowed with gigantic stature.

Primitive man's major preoccupation was to eke out his meager existence to the best of his ability and his survival was dependent to a very great extent on physical prowess. Life was unsettled and violent as he struggled against the harshness of conditions. A fearful respect for the elements, which to man were a series of inexplicable phenomena, came to involve the feverish worship of all sources of power. Thus his gods reflected his wonderment at the universe while giants both embodied the supreme physical strength he so envied and personified the most impressive of natural phenomena such as earthquakes, hurricanes and volcanic eruptions. His giants were supernatural beings of epic dimensions.

The fundamental accent on aggressive action and the fierce battling over domain and possessions are reflected in the earliest surviving legends which saw the giants and the gods in continuous conflict. Initially the giants were greatly feared, as few were considered to be kindly disposed to either men or gods. Legends passed – often fearfully – by word of mouth became an established part of the mythology, literature and folklore history of most of the peoples of the world.

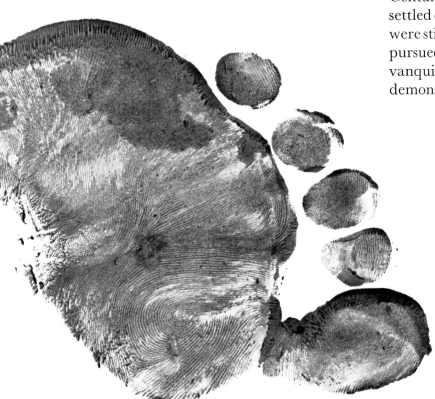

Centuries later man had, for the most part,
settled comfortably into communities. Giants
were still considered foes of society to be
pursued like other dangerous monsters and
vanquished in chivalrous adventures which
demonstrated the purported power of good over

evil. Blood-curdling tales of the evil deeds of gigantic men were related and subsequently incorporated into the great epic poems of the troubadours. Giants were believed to wield immense physical power backed by shrewd intelligence which enabled them to keep the man-sized population cowering at bay. Hence there were legends galore of maidens in distress rescued by giant-slaying knights in shining armor. Such tales fired noble listeners with wild enthusiasm for feats of heroism and flamboyant chivalry. The audience was held transfixed as a rich tapestry of action was slowly unfurled for their entertainment.

The colorful age of chivalry passed. As man became more aware of his own powers, he became less afraid of the unknown. Size lost its significance. Memories of bygone legends faded and giants were either relegated to the ranks of ridiculed freaks of nature or confined to the pages of children's stories.

Most giants were still seen as possessing great
strength and sturdiness although our researches
clearly indicate that they were quite frequently
plagued with physical ailments which rendered
their lives wearisome and painful. Paradoxically
many giants were whimsical and friendly rather
than aggressive and they often suffered curious
inferiority complex problems due to their
lumbering size. But we shall be examining these
areas more attentively in subsequent pages.

Who were these "giants"? Where did they come
from? To endeavor to answer these questions
we must consult the works of the earliest known
recorders of history – the artists, sculptors and
writers of antiquity. Naturally our interpretation
of this material is very personal but we feel that
it contributes a valuable insight into the
evolution of the world about us.

"And there we saw the giants, the sons of Anak, which come of the giants: and we were in our own sight as grasshoppers, and so we were in their sight."

(NUMBERS XIII. 33)

"And there was yet a battle in Gath, where was a man of great stature that had on every hand six fingers, and on every foot six toes, four and twenty in number; and he also was born to the giant."

(2 SAMUEL·XXI. 20)

Vivid illustrations and descriptions of giants and monsters by the sculptors, artists and writers of old were enhanced appreciably by exaggeration. In Palestine, memorials to primeval giants still exist in the form of vast graves. Noah's tomb in the Lebanon, for example, is seventy yards long. Huge on a different scale are Arthur's massive seat in Edinburgh and the chair of Gargantua on the Seine. Little wonder man marvels when he looks at the splendid remnants of antiquity: the sphinxes and pyramids of Egypt, the enormous temples and theaters of ancient Greece and Rome, the Druids' circles and the castles of England. Perplexed by the dimensions of such sites, early civilisations logically concluded that they had been constructed by giant ancestors.

Hence early and mediaeval man's fabulous accounts of peril and heroism must be taken with a large grain of salt as there was a tendency to glorify deeds and magnify stature out of pure admiration for bygone "heroes". The description "giant" was often assigned to personages who, although "gigantic" in terms of accomplishment (whether good or bad), were in fact of relatively normal stature. King Arthur is a prime example of this type of misrepresentation as were numerous other "great" men such as the fabled St. Christopher, Goliath – champion of the Philistines and Guy, Earl of Warwick. Yet other "giants" were, we fear, solely the product of gigantesque imaginations. While it is impossible to eliminate every apocryphal story, nevertheless we have endeavored to introduce restraint in our visual and narrative descriptions.

Relativity of size must also be taken into consideration. Anthropologists and medical specialists define a giant as being a person who stands over 1 ft 3 ins taller than the average member of his society. Clearly a native of the Watusi tribe (average height nearly seven feet) would seem immense to a pygmy. For this reason it is essential to distinguish between tall people and giants. After a very considerable research effort, the concerted opinion of the artists and writers involved in the production of this book is that the giant as *we* shall term him falls into two main categories: first there were the supernatural giants of antiquity (i.e. those existing in the half million years between the Creation and the Flood) and then there were the earthbound giants.

The painting on the facing page is the image of the giant as he sees himself — powerful, imposing and handsome. Unfortunately, the average giant was far more likely to look like this

Giants varied in size but were certainly beyond classification by human standards both in terms of size and power. For example the Book of Enoch relates that angels sent by God to guard the earth were seduced by the beauty of terrestrial women who subsequently gave birth to demoniacal sons 3,000 cubits* high. Later, ancient historians tell us, Og, the King of Bashan, who lived three thousand years, escaped the Flood by wading only knee-deep beside the Ark. He was able to roast a freshly caught fish by holding it up to the sun. Upon his death one of his bones was used as a bridge to span a river.

Attempting to destroy an Israelite camp, mighty Og ripped up a mountain six miles long at its base and bore it on his head on the trek towards the camp. Fortunately Moses, a comparative sprat merely ten cubits tall, jumped high into the air to strike Og on his forty-five foot high ankle with a ten-cubit long axe, thus felling and ultimately slaying his foe. Clearly reason casts doubt concerning the accuracy of these sizes. But in 1718 Abbé Henrion, a noted French academician, stressed that there had been a marked decrease in the height of men between the Creation and the Christian era. Henrion deduced that Adam was one hundred and thirty feet tall (despite early rabbinical writers' claims that Adam's head towered over the atmosphere and that his arms spanned the North and South poles). Henrion assigned a height of thirty feet to Abraham and (only) thirteen feet to Moses. Fortunately the advent of Christianity curtailed the shrinkage...

Earthbound species of giant ranged, by our calculations (and acknowledging exceptions), between forty five feet and ten feet – the latter of course pertaining to baby giants. In this context many well-known historical colossi (such as the "giant" knight Morholt slain by Tristan, the Green Knight vanquished by Sir Gawain and Lancashire's Sir Tarquin) regretfully must be considered as large men rather than giants.

That the size of the individual giant ran to a graduated scale with variations occurring more or less proportionately with those on the human scale would seem to be substantiated by Charles Darwin and Alfred Russell Wallace in their celebrated formal theory of evolution by natural selection. They noted that "the individuals in a

*A cubit represented the length of a man's arm from the tip of a finger to his elbow.

species are not all identical, but show variations in all characters." Subsequently, the authors observed that "therefore, some variants will succeed better and others less well in the competition for survival and the parents of the next generation will be naturally selected from among those members of the species that show variation in the direction of more effective adaptation to the conditions of their environment." The Darwin and Wallace theory provides a potential explanation for the gradual disappearance of giants.

The advent of inventions such as the wheel posed a serious threat to the presumed superiority of giants as advantages attached to size became redundant. As man gained in knowledge and ability, he began to mock giants. This led to the "freak" stigma which unfortunately has remained to this day. In the eighteenth century, giants were actually being exhibited to curious onlookers at county fairs. Initially some enterprising titans volunteered for this sort of supposed career but soon, overcome by indignity, returned to a life of relatively peaceful anonymity thereby leaving the field open to merely tall men.

A close examination of data pertaining to giants' general physical attributes and health resulted in some rather interesting conclusions. Early man's lack of psychological insight into the behavior patterns of giants led him to confuse physical enormity with aggression, strength and power. Although these gigantic beings appeared powerful in stature, they were frequently clumsy. The force of gravity starved their brains of essential blood supply, often rendering them slow-witted if not stupid.

Early writers (such as Homer in his description of the Cyclops* Polyphemus in the Odyssey) recognised that giants were often easily outwitted. The distance between the brain and the heart is a crucial factor and the lowering of the head below heart level could lead to blackouts and burst blood vessels. Poor circulation of the blood, particularly in the extremities, was also a general malaise of the species.

Note: Here we are talking of one "Cyclops" of the species "Cyclopes"

Giants were characterized by other rather useful physical features. Their arms were disproportionately long, often reaching just below the knees. This not only aided balance but also enabled giants to feel objects concealed by their protruding stomachs. The upper regions of their bodies were generally densely-forested with hair to aid survival in the damp swirling mists of the northern lowlands. Southern giants also tended to be hairy as this covering protected them from the burning sun and prevented excessive loss of body moisture. Some Nordic giants from the harshest climatic zones sprouted bushes and trees in their body hair for additional protection and camouflage – but more of this later.

Early manuscripts suggest that giants' ears and noses were long and downward-sloping to enable them to pick up the sounds and scents of the world far below. (Their ears were believed to have inspired the invention of the ear trumpet or original hearing aid.) These ears and noses were luxuriously furnished with thick tufts of hair to keep out cold mountain and sea breezes – as well as flocks of migrating birds. There was even one race of giants with wraparound ears.

Wraparound ears
are good for
winter protection

But in summer
months the
ears could be
bothersome
so with a
flick of the
neck and wrist
they were
knotted
together on
the top of
his head

Yet despite the protection of their hairy upper torsos, giants tended to be asthmatic, (interestingly this condition is often suffered by beings considered to be "insecure") in addition to suffering frequently from psychological problems such as feelings of inferiority, Oedipus Complexes and so forth.

However not all giants were afflicted with these unpleasant disorders. The healthier, wilier individuals often took advantage of human kindness by pretending to share their weaker compatriots' unfortunate plight, thereby contributing, however erroneously, to the generalization of the debility of the entire giant race.

But some characteristics were shared among virtually all giants. Their mouths, as well as other orifices, were very large. This enabled them to ingest the enormous quantities of nourishment required to feed their massive organisms. (Note that giants ate proportionately little, unlike very small animals such as mice who consume several times their body weight per day.)

We theorize that, owing to their heavy body weight, giants probably tended to slouch, resulting, in layman's terms, in pot-bellies, spare tyres and even collapsed rib-cages. Weight related conditions could have included various arterial malfunctions, varicose veins, haemorrhoids, flat feet, swollen joints (hence the frequent need for support bindings) and strokes. This leads the more pessimistic students of giantology to suggest that the knotted club traditionally wielded by giants was conceived of not as a weapon but rather as the precursor to today's shooting/walking stick . . . Rather unfortunately there seems to be a dearth of serious research data in this specific area.

Turning to temperament, giants were often rather pensive beings who could spend hours pondering a seemingly insoluble problem such as their age, the reason for their large size, the origins of light and darkness (a source of fear for most giants). Trolls were reportedly the most contemplative of the species.

Finally, some anthropologists have reported a drink problem among certain tribes, notably in northern regions. Did this alleged problem stem from physical discomfort and general depression or did giants simply enjoy the occasional tipple? Evidence points to their predilection for parties and other merrymaking when not up to mischief or pondering.

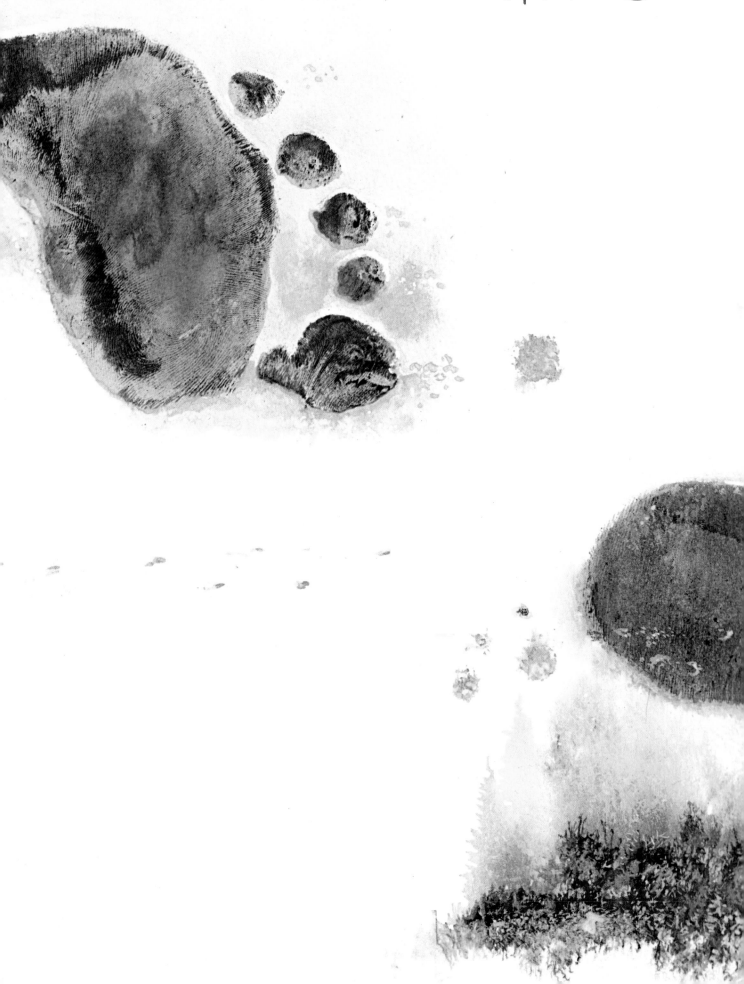

SUPERNATURAL GIANTS

Most mythologies relate that giants were the first living creatures to appear on the earth and that they preceded even the gods who were their sworn enemies. This enmity was founded on the gods' fear that the giants threatened their authority. Certainly the giants were envious of the power of the deities and did much to erode it, but curiously there was much fraternization between the races and several of the gods were reported to be the offspring of mixed unions.

Nevertheless there was continuous conflict between the giants and their progeny on one side and the various deities on the other. Man, the overawed spectator, lived in endless fear that an eventual widescale outbreak of hostilities would lead to a holocaust that would destroy the entire universe.

Norse Cosmology tells of Ginnungagap, the Great Void, which preceded the Creation. Ginnungagap consisted of Niflheim in the North, a region of dark and freezing fog, and Muspell in the South, an area engulfed by fire and flame. When the frozen wastes of the North met the fiery heat of the South, the first living creature was formed. This was a terrible giant named Ýmir, progenitor of the race of giants, whose left armpit begat a man and a woman while his two feet sired a family of frost-giants.

Ýmir was nourished by the milk of a cow by the name of Auðumbla from whose udders flowed four rivers of milk. Auðumbla in turn took sustenance from the salty ice-blocks of Ginnungagap. From one of these blocks emerged Búri, ancestor of the gods. Búri had a son, Bor, who married a giantess and the offspring of this union were the gods Óðin, Vili, and Ve. However, soon these three gods fell out with Ýmir and slew him. In his surging blood perished all the frost-giants save one, Bergelmir.

From Ýmir's body was formed the world of man. The giant's blood became the seas and lakes, his flesh the soil, his brains the clouds, his bones the mountains, his toes and teeth the rocks and boulders, his hair the vegetation. The gods fashioned the sky from the dome of his skull which was held up by the four dwarfs North, South, East and West who were maggots, bred inside Ýmir's carcass, to whom had been given human form and intelligence. The glowing cinders of Múspell were thrown up into the sky where they became the constellations. Finally the gods gave chariots and horses to a giantess called Night and to her son Day who ascended to the heavens and began to circle the earth once every twenty-four hours.

This world of men was called Miðgarð or Middle Earth and it was protected from the giants by a wall made from the eyebrows of Ýmir. Some sources insist that the man and woman born from Ýmir's armpit were the first inhabitants. Others relate how the gods created the first man from an ash tree and called him Aske, and the first woman from an alder and named her Embla . . .

At the center of the universe stood the World Tree, a mighty ash called Yggdrasil which sprang from the corpse of Ýmir. Yggdrasil had three massive roots. One of these extended into the land of the gods which was known as Ásgarð; another reached into Jötunheim, the abode of the giants; the third extended into icy Niflheim which had become the realm of death. At the roots of Yggdrasil lay a fount of wisdom. This was tended by the giant Mímir who was reputed to be so wise that even Óðin, the Alfaður or All-Father of gods, would approach him for advice.

Ásgarð was carefully guarded against the frost and mountain giants and access was only possible across the bridge Bifröst, the rainbow. By this rainbow bridge dwelt Heimdall, the white god, whose task it was to act as sentry. So anxious were the gods to protect their realm from incursion by giants that they once rashly promised a mountain giant the sun and the moon—as well as the hand of the exquisite goddess Freya – if he could construct a massive wall around Ásgarð within a given time. The gods agreed to the giant's proposal because they considered the feat impossible to accomplish within the time limit. They were content with the thought that they could gain a welcome extra protective edifice without effort on their part. However, the giant owned a wondrous horse called Svaðilfari with whose aid the wall soon neared completion. The gods were furious and treacherously lured away the giant's steed, thus thwarting the giant's efforts to accomplish his task. Thór, implacable adversary of the giant race, then slew the unfortunate builder with his magic hammer, Mjöllnir.

The most splendid of all the gold and silver palaces of the gods in Ásgarð was Valhöll, the hall of the slain. Here Óðin royally fêted those who had fallen bravely in battle. When not feasting, these heroes amused themselves in combat by hacking each other to pieces. Yet as dusk fell the slain rose again to feast anew. Óðin gathered these warriors about him in preparation for the day of reckoning when they would rise up against their foes, the giants, in a final battle on the plain of Vigrið.

Like the giants, the gods had most of the faults of man. Envy, greed and malice were dangerous emotions when bolstered by supernatural powers. One semi-deity, Loki, was particularly renowned for his treachery. Although the son of a giant and father by his union with the giantess Angrboða (Distress-Bringer) of three horrific monsters – the wolf Fenrir, Hel (Death) and the World Serpent (Miðgarðsorm) – he aligned himself with the gods. Loki delighted in creating dangerous situations which threatened Ásgarð, presumably so that he could then demonstrate his prowess at extricating the gods at the last moment. Loki was particularly adept at spreading spurious rumours and was renowned for his malicious character. Inexplicably the gods tolerated him until he caused the death of Óðin's favorite son, Baldur. Loki fled from his fate but the gods caught him and bound him with chains. A serpent was suspended over his head in such a way that it dripped venom on his face, drop by drop. Although Loki's faithful wife Sigyn sat at his side to catch the drops in a cup, periodically she was obliged to empty it. Then the venom fell on Loki, making him writhe and scream with horror and this, in turn, caused the whole earth to quake.

Loki's treachery was once nearly Thór's undoing. Loki was flying about disguised as Freya when he was captured by the giant Geirroð. Geirroð recognized Loki by his eyes, locked him up and starved him for three months until he promised to trick Thór into coming to Geirroð's abode without his mighty hammer or his belt of strength. Loki did this but Thór was warned of the trap by a friendly giantess who lent him her magic staff, iron gloves and another belt.

One of Geirroð's daughters attempted to drown Thór by blocking a stream to make it swell but Thór managed to fell her with a huge boulder. Then Thór entered into Geirroð's huge hall and sat down to rest. He suddenly felt himself lifted by Geirroð's other two daughters and was in danger of being crushed against the roof. Thór forced the seat down with the help of his borrowed magic staff and in so doing broke the giantesses' backs. Geirroð made a last desperate attempt to slay the god, flinging a ball of hot iron at him. But Thór caught the ball with his iron gloves and threw it back so fiercely that it demolished the pillar concealing Geirroð and killed the giant.

A FROST GIANT

The Death of Ymir

Another god considered to be of the giant race was Aegir, ruler of the sea. However Aegir posed no threat to the gods and indeed made an appreciable contribution to their well-being by his other function as Ale-Brewer. His links with the giants were his nine daughters, the waves of the sea. These he called by such names as Gjolp (Howler) and Greip (Grasper) which were typical names for giantesses. Legend has it that Heimdall, the white god, was born of the sea and

fostered by nine giantesses, popularly believed to be the daughters of Aegir. An Irish saga also tells the story of nine sea giantesses who mothered a boy among them after capturing Ruad, son of Rigdonn, as he crossed the seas to Norway.

When Ruad broke his promise to return to see his son at the end of his voyage, the furious giantesses cut off the head of the child and hurled it in the direction of the disappearing ship.

A sworn enemy of the giant race was Thór, the God of Thunder, whose mighty hammer, Mjöllnir, cracked many a giant's skull. The giant Thrym once stole Thór's hammer and buried it eight fathoms deep in Jötunheim. Thór sent Loki to negotiate with Thrym but the giant would only consent to return the hammer if he were granted the hand of the lovely goddess Freya in exchange. So Thór disguised himself as the goddess and, veiled appropriately, journeyed to Jötunheim accompanied by Loki. He remained undiscovered and when the giant honored his pledge to return the hammer, Thor threw off his disguise and slaughtered Thrym and all his following.

On one occasion a giant called Hrungnir unwisely visited Ásgarð uninvited, became very drunk and boasted that he intended to destroy Ásgarð in order to carry off the most beautiful of the goddesses. Thór was summoned and challenged Hrungnir. Hrungnir pointed out that he was without his shield and whetstone but that he was quite willing to engage in single combat at a later date. After the duel was arranged, the wily giants fashioned a decoy clay giant to divert Thór's attention and thus enable Hrungnir to deal with him. However when one of Thór's companions discovered the plot, he cunningly told Hrungnir that Thór intended to attack from under the ground, advising Hrungnir to lay his shield on the ground beneath him. When Thór arrived he demolished the clay giant in an instant and hurled his hammer at Hrungnir who in turn threw his whetstone at Thór with all his might. The two weapons met in mid-air: the whetstone shattered and fragments pierced Thór's head so that he fell dazed to the ground; the hammer meanwhile hit Hrungnir's stone forehead, crushing his head to dust, resulting in the giant falling dead on top of Thór. None of the gods was able to free Thór but soon Thór's infant son Magni (Might), arrived and, despite his tender age (he was three days old at the time), he tossed the giant's body aside. Thór recovered his senses and returned home triumphant.

On another occasion the god Thór, accompanied by Loki, Thialfi and Roskva decided to visit the castle of Útgarðar-Loki in Jötunheim. One evening as the gods were en route to their destination, they resolved to stop for the night. Observing a great hall with a massive entrance along one side, Thór and his companions chose this as their resting place but, unbeknownst to them, the hall was in fact a giant's glove. During the night they were roused by a terrifying earthquake which was none other than the snoring of the sleeping giant, whose name was Skrymir. The size of the giant whom they discovered the next morning so startled Thór that, apart from attempting thrice in vain to shatter the dozing Skrymir's skull with his mighty hammer Mjöllnir, he realistically decided to abandon his efforts to vanquish the giant and prudently continued his journey to the castle of Útgarðar-Loki.

As the travellers departed, Skrymir warned them that they were approaching Útgarðar-Loki's kingdom—the domain of giants even more powerful than he. On their arrival Thór and his entourage were challenged to a contest with their hosts. Despite the greatest efforts of the gods, their prodigious powers seemed insignificant when pitted against those of their giant adversaries. Just as his disillusioned guests were about to leave, Útgarðar-Loki disclosed to Thór that the latter's defeat was only illusory—he, Útgarðar-Loki, was also the giant Skrymir and he had been horrified by Thór's strength which doubtless would have destroyed his kingdom had it not been for certain tricks he had employed: the blows struck at Skrymir's head by Thór's hammer Mjöllnir had been diverted to the plane of the earth which was now scarred by three mighty valleys; the adversary in an eating contest had been all-devouring fire; Útgarðar-Loki's representative in a track event had been Thought itself; a horn proffered to Thór in a drinking contest had had its tip in the ocean; and Thór's opponent in a wrestling match was none other than Old Age. Thór was so incensed at being deceived by such trickery that he resolved to shatter Útgarðar-Loki into tiny pieces but, as he raised his hammer, both the giant king and his entire kingdom disappeared.

The story of Odin
and the magic mead...

There was intense competition for possessions between the giants and the gods. The jealous giants hankered after the numerous treasures of Ásgarð and stole what they could. The mountain giant Süttung managed to appropriate from the dwarfs a magic mead, the potion of poetry and learning. This he carefully buried under his mountain. But the god Óðin changed himself into a serpent, and having burrowed his way down to the precious fluid, he convinced Süttung's daughter to allow him to drink from the treasured casks of mead. These he emptied in three long draughts. Then, transforming himself into an eagle he flew off to Ásgarð. Süttung set off in furious pursuit, also in the form of an eagle. But as the gods saw Óðin approaching, they set out vats by the walls of Ásgarð and Óðin quickly regurgitated the mead before Süttung could catch him.

Nordic myths foretold that the endless feud between gods and giants would lead to Ragnarök, a day of doom which would witness the almost total destruction of the universe and the end of all the giants. Three terrible winters in succession would herald the day of disaster when seas would boil, the earthquakes would rip the earth, all the forces of evil would be unleashed and the dead would rise. The giants of Múspell, led by Surt the Fire Giant, would ride forth from the south and join the frost and mountain-giants, the legions of the dead and the monsters of land and sea in a final horrendous battle against the gods.

However the myths foresaw that after the slaughter all evil would be destroyed. Only two sons of Óðin and two sons of Thór would survive to rebuild Ásgarð. In the World Tree, the sole remaining entity, would cower two mortals, a man and a woman destined to repopulate the earth when it arose green and fertile from beneath the waters. And eventually the god Baldur would return from the dead to lead a new golden age.

Yggdrasil
the
World
Tree

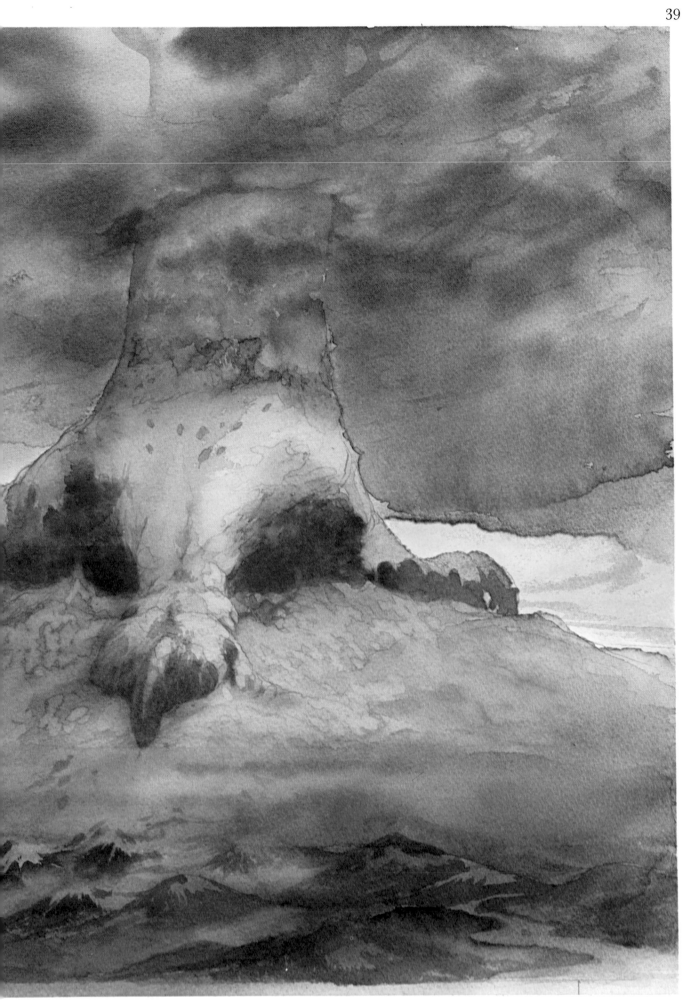

A tribe of North American Indians believes that the first human beings on the earth were a race of gigantic Indians—so large that even the mighty buffalo was dwarfed by their size. Such a giant Indian could lift a full-grown buffalo bull from the ground and throw it over his shoulder, carrying it back to his encampment effortlessly. A yearling to him was so small he would simply hang it from his belt as a hunter today might do with a rabbit.

These giant forebears had no fear of any superior power, had no notion of a life after death and did not believe in Ti-ra'-wa, the all powerful one who watches over the destiny of man. So the giants did as they pleased with no regard for the consequences. Finally, when the deeds they perpetrated had reached unacceptable proportions, Ti-ra'-wa resolved to punish the big men. He caused the waters of the rivers, lakes and seas to rise up until they were level with the land. The ground became soft and the heavy giants sank down into the mud and were drowned. Even today massive bones are still found in remoter areas of North America.

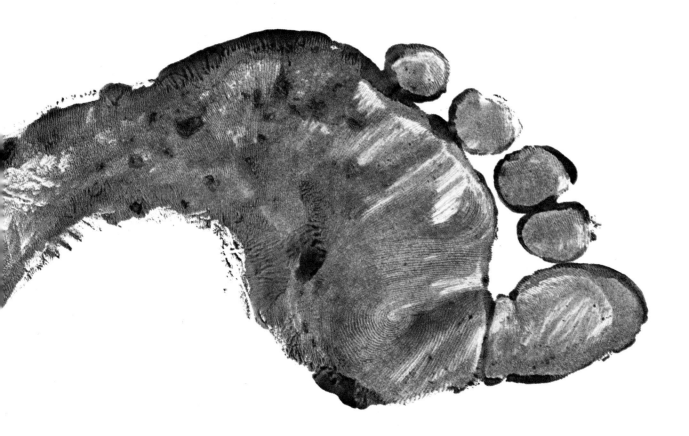

THE EARTHLY GIANTS

" . . . a legendary manlike being of more than
mortal but less than godlike power and
endowment. A person of unusual stature or
size." (WEBSTER)

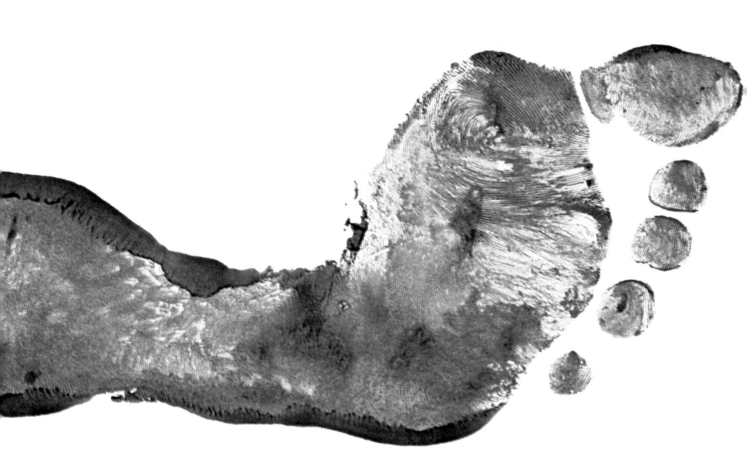

Although the earthly giants were not faced with such formidable adversaries as the gods, they had to contend in many cases with the uncomprehending hostility of man. Originally this hostility was understandable to a large extent. Giants had a tendency to take themselves rather too seriously. Their ancient rôle as the supernatural originator of mankind probably left them with an overdeveloped feeling of self-importance. They had always attempted to "pull rank" where the gods were concerned (hence the irritated defensiveness of these powerful deities) and the earthly titans had a misguided sense of responsibility towards man who, however, responded aggressively through resentment, ignorance or fear.

While the big men soon overcame their initial superiority complex over man, man himself is historically more inclined towards prejudice. Admittedly early man revered the giant for his size and saw him as a powerful fertility symbol. Rock and hill carvings, ancient rites involving wicker giant effigies—all these point to an historic reverence for the giant. Indeed a veritable giant cult existed at certain periods of history. The advent of Christianity, however, changed all this. The giant rapidly became an outcast. Hated and feared for being different, in the eyes of man he was equated with the devil. There was also confusion between giants and monsters (hence the erroneous impression that ogres such as the horrific Grendel and his even more repulsive mother in *Beowulf* were giants). Such beliefs led to widespread feeling that giants were inherently evil.

Later, although man was less ignorant, the mediaeval love of ordered ceremony, ornament and delicate sensitivity precluded such cumbersome hulks from normal society. The parallel joys of chivalry and fierce aggression made the giant an ideal beast of prey — second only to the dragon.

" There were giants
in the earth in those days "
(GENESIS VI, 4)

ON LEGENDARY BELIEFS:

Doubtless many, if not most, of the valleys and gorges to be found in the more mountainous regions of the world can fairly be attributed to the colossal weight of giants traipsing about while the earth's crust was still soft. However, stories that it was giant tears that filled some gorges to form rivers and streams are of course false as is the quite widespread belief that the big people could only move about in the dark as a single ray of sunlight would turn them to stone—if the latter theory were true it would disprove numerous authenticated reported sightings and would certainly pose the question—how on earth did creatures of such lumbering size avoid wreaking total havoc as they fumbled around in the dark .. ? The sole credible exception to this rule are giants from the northernmost reaches who, of course, are well used to months of darkness. The theory that many giants were sensitive to sunlight probably arose as a result of migrations of northern giants to other shores. We know for example that the Norwegians brought a number of their giants with them to Orkney and Shetland and Ernest W. Marwick has recorded that "These giants continued to do the things that they, or their ancestors, had done in Norway. They quarrelled, and threw boulders at each other, they set huge isolated rocks in the sea close to shore so that they could sit on them and fish; they hated to get their feet wet, and tried to build bridges from island to island, often unsuccessfully; they stayed out too long at night and were turned into stone by beams of the morning sun".

The mighty constructions of former giants further disprove such fallacies—building in the dark, even with the aid of flares, would have proven a very hazardous task. While it might have been possible to manage, albeit with difficulty, where giant roads or castles were concerned, other edifices were built on less than stable terrain. The Giant's Causeway, for example, a promontory on the north coast of County Antrim in Northern Ireland, was extended by the giants across the sea to Scotland and was used for many years as a route for giant travellers. (What became of this very logical extension is unknown.)

The travel factor is, in fact, an important point in our study of giants. Like man, giants were not equally spread numerically across the world from the beginning. Giants were as much a prey to the whims of nature, natural disasters and disease as man. Successive migrations characterized the early days as all beings strove to find a habitat which provided the essentials for life. Obviously the world then was not entirely as we know it today. Some continents now separate were joined. Luxurious forests have given way to arid deserts. Where there were oceans separating man from his goal, the mystery of his crossings has largely been solved. In the case of the giants, however, it is difficult to imagine the creation of reed craft or even balsawood rafts large enough to serve as vessels.

PROOF

Throughout history seemingly conclusive evidence for the existence of giants has been submitted by eminent scientists. Although certain established theories have been rejected by archaeologists and palaeontologists in order to make way for new "discoveries", other findings have weathered the attacks of the critics and merit discussion.

Of the many discoveries of ancient bones of epic proportions believed to date from periods as early as the Tertiary Era through the Pleistocene Era to the Ice Age, three findings of fossilized remains are particularly significant to thinking concerning the origins of giants: Gigantopithecus Blacki (popularly known as the Kwangsi Giant), Meganthropus Palaeojavanicus (Java Man) and Meganthropus Africanus.

These discoveries led to the development of two different schools of thought. The first theory is that originally there were two distinct types of men—giants and "men of brain". The thinking here was that whereas giants possessed bodies more acclimatized to the harsh existence of the Ice Age, they lost their usefulness as conditions improved; eventually the "men of brain" completely displaced the giants, culminating in the latter's gradual extinction.

The second theory is that man as we now know him is descended from a race of giants. In support of either theory, experts have concluded that the "Dragon's Teeth" commonly sold in Chinese pharmacies for their curative properties are in fact the remains of primeval giants. Meanwhile, in numerous other countries, archaeologists have unearthed utensils of such enormous size that they could only have been used by giants. Even more obvious evidence remains in the way of traditions passed down through the ages. In many countries (notably Britain, France, Belgium and the Netherlands) summer-time festivals were celebrated with processions led by huge wicker giants. A sixteenth-century author, George Puttenham, described "midfommer pageants in London, where to make the people wonder are fet forth great and vglie Gyants marching as if they were aliue, and armed at all points, but within they are ftuffed full of browne paper and tow, which the fhrewd boyes vnder-peering do guilefully difcouer and turne to a great derifion:" Sometimes these effigies were burned—yet another symbol of man's continual conflict with the men of brawn.

Many giant sightings have been reported in the Himalayas

There is also
a wealth of
traces of giants
to be found in
the open countryside
and these again
are generally characterized
by rather conspicuous
dimensions.
Such traces include
landmarks, structures
and hill figures
but these we shall
be examining more
closely in later
pages.

Certain locations are particularly renowned for archaeological discoveries pointing to the existence of giants. Patagonia is one such area as is Sicily where so many supernatural giants met their fate. As early as the fourteenth century at Trapani in Sicily, Giovanni Boccaccio, celebrated author of the Decameron, unearthed a collection of fossilized bones which included a gigantic skull with a huge hole located just under the forehead. The Greek philosopher Empedocles had already mentioned such finds and had referred to them as the "bones of Polyphemus". Boccaccio was of the same opinion.

Far earlier, during the time of Pliny, an earthquake on the Greek island of Crete resulted in a fissure in a mountain which revealed a skeleton measuring 46 cubits in length.

In 1936, a French-led archaeological expedition to Chad in Africa unearthed a number of egg-shaped funeral jars containing the remains of a gigantic race in addition to jewellery and pieces of art. (This is a clear indication that traditional descriptions of the giants as a lumbering crew of slow-witted idlers are suspect.)

Patagonia for its part may even have derived its very name from the very large feet (patas) of one of the rather elevated Indian tribes who ruled over the region in past days. It was in the late fifteenth/early sixteenth century, indeed a golden age of discovery, that giants were encountered frequently by explorers wending their perilous way from continent to continent. Ferdinand Magellan (c. 1480-1521), the famed Portuguese leader of the first expedition to circumnavigate the globe, was amazed at the gigantic stature of a Tehuelche Indian he saw dancing on the shore when he arrived at San Julián in 1520. Rather highhandedly he decided to kidnap a couple of giants to take back to Europe with him as souvenirs. He tricked his prey into allowing their ankles to be shackled. One of these giants was fortunate enough to escape but the other was taken aboard one of Magellan's ships. Out in mid-Pacific, this unfortunate being soon died of scurvy.

Two centuries previously the Venetian Marco Polo (1254-1324) had brought back stories of giants from his travels in the East.

Such reported sightings could be taken to
corroborate either of the two aforesaid theories.
Certainly they do indicate that giants, like
men, vary in appearance according to habitat.
The Patagonian giants had a far darker
pigmentation than, say, that of a troll in
Northern Norway, while eastern giants
reportedly had all the physical characteristics of
an easterner today.

APPEARANCE

THE FIRST BATTLE OF BRITAIN

"Eald enta geweorc īdlu stōdon"

(from *The Wanderer*, an
Old English elegy from
The Exeter Book).

In the beginning Britain was occupied by a fearsome tribe of giants. These were the offspring of Lady Albine and her thirty-two sisters who were the daughters of the Emperor Dioclesian. Caxton's *Chronicle of England* tells us that with great difficulty the Emperor managed to marry off all his daughters. However, as they were unhappy at the loss of their personal liberty, the thirty-three together conspired to murder their unfortunate husbands. And so they did.

The infuriated Emperor decided he could no longer cope with his wilful offspring and he ordered them to be cast adrift at sea with sufficient provisions for six months' sailing. The evil crew discovered and settled on an island which they named after Lady Albine's son, Albion.

In *Chronicles of Great Britain*, written in the mid-fifteenth century, John de Wavrin relates that the devil moved in among these ladies. As a result a race of particularly nasty giants and giantesses was born. These multiplied and for a while were the sole occupiers of the land.

Enter Brutus, the younger son of Anthenor of Troy. Accompanied by a party of Trojan exiles under the leadership of a champion fighter called Corineus, Brutus landed at what is now the port of Southampton. Lady Albine's son, Albion, after whom the island was named, heard of the invasion and "raised his whole power, being men of gigantick stature, and vast strength, and bearing for their arms huge clubs of knotty oak, battle axes, whirlbats of iron, and globes full of spikes, fastened to a long pole by a chain; and with these encountered Brute, a bloody battle was fought, wherein the Trojans were worsted and many of them slain, and their

whole army was forced to retire." (from *The History of the Trojan Wars and Troy's Destruction* 1735). But Brutus was not one to give up easily. During the night a long, deep trench was dug and lines of sharp stakes were driven into its floor. A network of leafy branches covered with dried leaves and earth concealed the trench. The giants were then challenged to a second battle. The ensuing events can well be imagined. Suffice it to say the Trojans emerged victorious and the remaining giants fled to Cornwall, hotly pursued by Brutus's men. At this point Brutus decided it would be a wise idea to divide the island in two as this would facilitate control of the titanic natives. Cornwall he gave to Corineus, keeping the remainder of Albion under his rule and renaming it Britain.

In a subsequent bloody battle Albion was slain by Brutus while his brother Gogmagog, the mightiest of the giants in Britain, was killed by the warrior Corineus who hurled the monster over a cliff. This cliff was henceforth known as Lan-Goemagog or the Giant's Leap.

Another version of this story claims there were two giants called Gog and Magog who were more powerful than all the others. Vanquished in battle, they were taken prisoner and "led in triumph to the place where now London stands," and Brutus . . . "upon those risings on the side of the river Thames, founded a city, which he called Troy-novant, or New Troy, and building a palace where Guildhall stands, caused the two giants to be chained to the gate of it, as porters. In memory of which it is held that their effigies, after their deaths, were set up as they now appear in Guildhall." In fact the statues dubbed Gog and Magog at the Guildhall in London represented the conquered Gogmagog and his conqueror Corineus.

Despite the efforts of Brutus to rid Britain of its giants, some managed to survive—fortunately for our civilization as their accomplishments have proven that for every bad giant there was at least one whose valuable services far outshadowed the evil perpetrated by less benevolent titans.

Take for example Bendegeit Bran, or Bran the Blessed as he was sometimes known. This giant man was one of the very earliest Kings of Britain,* the Isle of the Mighty. His feats are recorded in *The Mabinogion*, that famed and valuable collection of mediaeval Welsh tales which firmly places him among the greatest heroes of his era.

As was fitting for a man of his position, Bendegeit Bran was of such gigantic stature that in his kingdom no house could be built large enough to accommodate him, nor ship stout enough to carry him.

Bendegeit Bran had a sister Branwen of whom he was very fond. Nevertheless, political expediency dictated that Branwen should be betrothed to the King of Ireland, one Matholwch. Sadly this monarch was somewhat weak in character and had a regrettable tendency to listen to his more disreputable courtiers. To cut a fascinating story short, such feebleness led King Matholwch to mistreat his wife shamefully, consigning her to turn the spit in his kitchens where she was subjected to continual buffeting and other humiliations.

Eventually Branwen found a way to advise her brother of her plight and he gathered his forces immediately to speed to the rescue. Striding through the sea, Bendegeit Bran, King of Britain, himself pulled his ships swiftly to Ireland so that short-sighted Irish lookouts were confounded at the sight of a floating forest (ships' masts) drawing near beside a huge mountain (Bran) from which jutted a lofty ridge with a lake on either side (the giant's nose and eyes).

Panic stricken when they understood what this curious sight meant, the Irish beat a hasty retreat across the river Llinon, destroying as they went the only bridge to ford that river. Once across the rushing waters, the Irish believed themselves to be safe, as the Llinon boasted the curious characteristic of a riverbed of magnetic stones which impeded the progress of any vessel. But wily King Bran simply lay down, stretching himself out from bank to bank, acting as a bridge for his armies.

When the Irish King saw that all was lost, he effected a tricky truce with the British, offering to build Bendegeit Bran a huge house as a peace token. But on either side of each of the one hundred pillars supporting the house was hung a hide bag and in every bag crouched a fully-armed warrior . . .

Note: In those times Britain comprised Lloegr or England, Cymry (later Cymru) or Wales and Alban or Scotland.

King Bran was no simpleton however—his fame was founded on shrewd action; he drew close to a bag and demanded of a nearby Irishman to know its contents. "Flour", replied the enemy. Bendegeit Bran felt around the contours of the bag and came across the head of the hidden warrior—this he squeezed until his fingers met through the skull. And so he did with the other one hundred and ninety-nine bags and even an armored head could not deter him . . .

Of no less regal stature in *The Mabinogion*, although a somewhat less favorable aura surrounds him, is Ysbaddaden, Chief-giant of the domain of giants and father of the beautiful Olwen. Basically he was reproached with an over-protective attitude towards his daughter although closer inspection of his reasoning leads to understanding—Ysbaddaden was fated to die when Olwen took a husband. Thus the Chief-giant acquired a reputation for disposing of all suitors to his daughter's hand.

A certain Culhwch, of noble blood and a cousin to King Arthur, had a spell cast on him which inflamed him with love for Olwen although he had never seen her. Recruiting the help of his cousin Arthur, he set off for the Chief-giant's fort. Meeting a giant herdsman in the vicinity of the fort, Culhwch explained his mission. Dire warnings could not dissuade Culhwch in his determination, so it came about that he and his supporters managed to enter the fort . . .

The Chief-giant three times endeavored to kill this new suitor with poisoned spears—and three times the visitors caught and returned the spears which embedded themselves respectively in the giant's knee-cap, breast and eyeball. The furious giant then resorted to a clever ruse. He demanded that Culhwch accomplish a staggering number of seemingly impossible feats against potentially invincible odds. Yet all this Culhwch in his ardor managed to accomplish with the help of Arthur's court. And so Culhwch won the hand of his love and Ysbaddaden the Chief-giant relinquished his life.

Although the fertile imaginations of early writers endowed many heroes with gigantic size, there is a solid basis for Dr Pritchard's remark in his *History of Mankind*: "In Ireland men of uncommon stature are often seen, and even a gigantic form and stature occur there much more frequently than in this island: yet all the British isles derived their stock of inhabitants from the same sources. We can hardly avoid the conclusion that there must be some peculiarity in Ireland which gives rise to these phenomena." Whether weather, diet or latitude were responsible, certainly accounts of the deeds of such redoubtable giants as Fingall (or Fuen-vie-Couil, or Fin McCoul) and his son Ossian (or Ussheen) leave no doubt as to the basis for such speculation. It was Fingall and his gigantic relatives who built the Giant's Causeway.

As a young boy, the giant Fingall fell into the clutches of a far more powerful giant who forced him into service. This giant had sought in vain for a salmon with the gift of prophecy. For seven long years young Fingall served him and finally the giant caught the treasured salmon. This he gave to Fingall to roast with dire warnings of his fate should anything untoward occur. But young Fingall allowed his mind to wander as he roasted the fish over the fire. A large blister arose on one side of the salmon. Aghast the boy tried to press this down with his thumb. In so doing he burnt his finger and popping it into his mouth he suddenly realized he had gained the knowledge the giant so desired.

Fleeing in fear, the boy was soon hotly pursued by the giant. But each time he was in danger of being caught his finger would smart, he would pop it into his mouth to cool it, and would realize how to make good his escape.

Years later Fingall was happily married and his wife Oonagh had borne him a fine son. A certain Scottish giant named Cucullin meanwhile had heard tell of Fingall's prowess and he determined to discover which of them might prove the stronger. Fingall's gift of knowledge enabled him to foresee this threat to his peaceful existence and his wife Oonagh was swift to find a solution. She baked a number of large loaves, concealing in the centre of the largest one the griddle she had used in making the bread. Then she boiled quantities of milk, separating the curds and whey and forming the curds into a solid mass. Oonagh then disguised her husband as a baby and popped him into a cradle.

On the arrival of the Scottish giant, Oonagh explained that her husband was absent but bid him await his return. In good housewifely manner, Oonagh offered her visitor the largest loaf. Cucullin bit into this but understandably had difficulty in biting through it so he placed it aside. Then the giant asked Oonagh what was her husband's favorite feat of strength; she answered that it was to squeeze water out of a stone lying near the door. The visitor immediately took up the stone and squeezed it with all his might and until his fingers bled but not a drop of water appeared. At this Oonagh mocked the big man, saying that even a child could do better. Handing her "baby" the lump of curds, she encouraged him to squeeze it and a few drops of whey fell to the floor ...

Next the fond mother broke off a piece of bread and gave this to her "baby"—he devoured it with relish. Amazed the visiting Scot asked how on earth the child could eat such hard bread. Oonagh persuaded the giant to put his finger into the "baby's" mouth to feel its teeth and at this her husband bit off the finger. This was too much for the Scottish giant—seeing the strength of Fingall's child, he did not wait to meet the father but took himself back to Scotland as fast as his feet could carry him.

TRACES

"Jack the giant had nothing to do,
So he made a hedge from Lerrin to Looe."
(traditional rhyme)

That giants often put their strength to constructive use was, and still is, evident. Even the rather infamous Cyclopes (Polyphemus excepted) were renowned for their fantastic edifices.

"These stones are connected with certain secret religious rites and they have various properties which are medicinally important. Many years ago the Giants transported them from the remotest confines of Africa and set them up in Ireland at a time when they inhabited that country. Their plan was that, whenever they felt ill, baths should be prepared at the foot of the stones; for they used to pour water over them and to run this water into baths in which their sick were cured. What is more, they mixed the water with herbal concoctions and so healed their wounds. There is not a single stone among them which hasn't some medicinal virtue."
(The History of the Kings of Britain— GEOFFREY OF MONMOUTH)

Giants with magical powers were, it is often believed, responsible for the transport from Africa to Ireland of the massive bluestones destined for Stonehenge. Merlin then used his secret powers to bring these stones to England, flying with them over the Irish Sea and depositing them at Amesbury. Other giants must have then dragged them to nearby Stonehenge and arranged them in the formation so well known today.

There are, of course, numerous conflicting theories as to the true origin of these stones but what is conclusive is this: while the sarsen blocks of Stonehenge could have been quarried in north Wiltshire, bluestones were not available locally—the nearest possible source being South Wales or Ireland. Hence journeys over land and possibly water were entailed. Such a task would logically demand the recruitment of giants.

Rocks and boulders played an exceedingly important part in giant life. According to size (either that of the giant or the rock) they were playthings, weapons, means of camouflage, seats, quoits, bowls, marbles and, on a more mundane level, building materials. Remnants of giant activity of this sort are still to be seen, dotted across the length and breadth of the British Isles as well as in innumerable other places in the world.

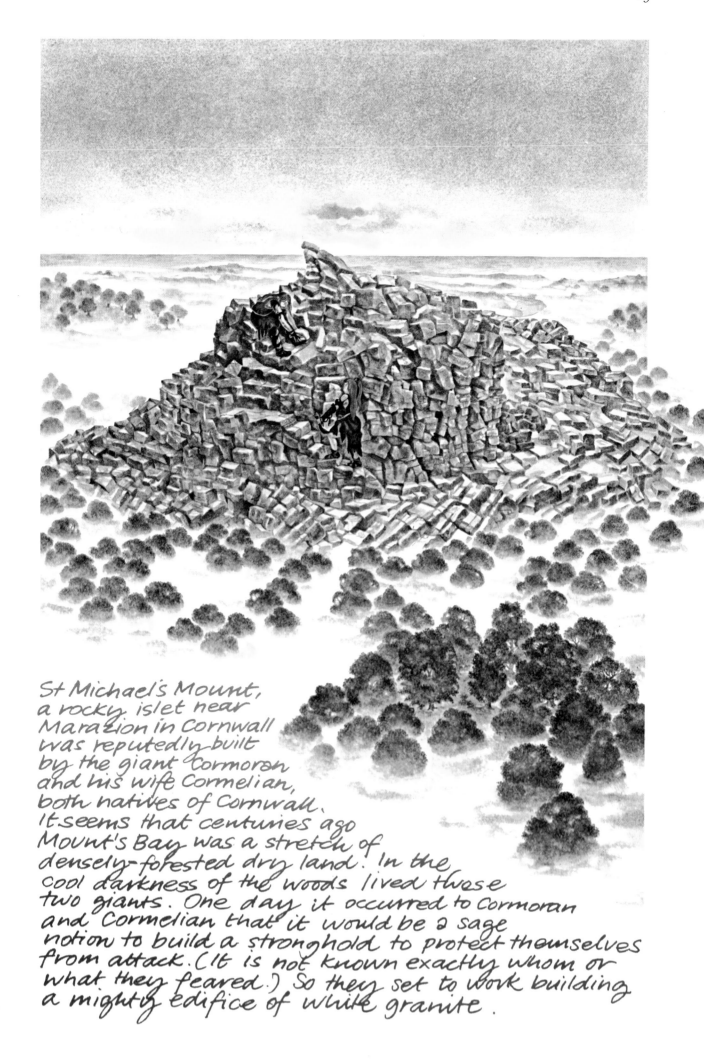

St Michael's Mount,
a rocky islet near
Marazion in Cornwall
was reputedly built
by the giant Cormoran
and his wife Cormelian,
both natives of Cornwall.
It seems that centuries ago
Mount's Bay was a stretch of
densely-forested dry land. In the
cool darkness of the woods lived those
two giants. One day it occurred to Cormoran
and Cormelian that it would be a sage
notion to build a stronghold to protect themselves
from attack. (It is not known exactly whom or
what they feared.) So they set to work building
a mighty edifice of white granite.

Now Cormoran was a rather lazy giant by nature and at one point, when his wife was not looking, he settled down for a short nap. Soon Cormelian noticed her husband sunk in peaceful slumber. Cunningly she decided to collect the odd greenstone rock rather than white granite as this entailed a shorter journey. But, as she lugged her first greenstone along in her apron Cormoran awoke to catch his wife red-handed. Angrily he aimed a hefty kick at Cormelian. Her apron strings snapped with a mighty twang and the rock she was carrying tumbled to the ground where it has remained to this day, forming the causeway leading to St. Michael's Mount.

The sight of a giant raising himself up
unexpectedly after a quick snooze on a hillside
was quite impressive enough to have inspired
the cult for hill figures that flowered among early
cultures on the British Isles. The best known of
these include the Long Man of Wilmington in
Sussex, the Cerne Abbas giant in Dorset and the
Uffington Horse in Berkshire.

Local legend has it that the gigantic hill figure at Cerne Abbas depicts a Danish giant. However, the way in which his outline was preserved for posterity has its gory side. It seems this giant led an invasion of Britain – a tiring task as, when he reached the hill, he lay down for a rapid forty winks. The local people, rather incensed at this "foreign" presence on their hill, crept up on the sleeping giant and cut off his head, leaving his impression on the hillside as a warning to any other intending invaders.

An early giant
observed men
and their use
of horses—
he then tried
to attract a
likely beast
to his hill.

The giant of Grabbist in Somerset was a gentle giant most of the time— but by no means all of the time. Once the Devil himself was imprudent enough to tangle with him by cheating at a stone-lobbing competition. Beelzebub found himself lifted into the air by his tail and tossed ignominiously into the Bristol Channel.

The giant of Grabbist became very popular
with the local people. At a time when the coast
was plagued with smugglers, wreckers and
pirates, this giant assumed the rôle of one-man
life-brigade for local small craft. The *Dorcas
Jane* was one boat that nearly foundered off the
Somerset coast until the giant of Grabbist came
to her rescue.

The Wrekin hill in Shropshire owes its existence to an unfriendly Welsh giant. This particular fellow bore a grudge against the mayor and townsfolk of Shrewsbury and he conceived a nasty plan to make his feelings felt. He decided to dam the river Severn to cause a flood which would drown them all. Fortunately for Shrewsbury, this giant was not endowed with a particularly accurate sense of direction. He managed to lose himself completely as he trudged towards where he thought the town should lie. The giant was soon thoroughly hot and bothered, principally because he was carrying a large spadeful of earth destined for the Severn. He came across a cobbler and asked the man in which direction Shrewsbury lay. The cobbler, curious, asked the giant his mission and in reply the giant disclosed his plan.

Now the cobbler had many customers in Shrewsbury whom he was loath to lose. Indeed he was en route for home from the town bearing a sack of shoes and boots for cobbling. The cobbler showed the giant his sack and warned "You'll never get to Shrewsbury, not today, nor tomorrow. Why, look at me! I'm just come from Shrewsbury, and I've had time to wear out all these old boots and shoes on the road since I started." (From Charlotte Burne's *Shropshire Folk-lore.*) Thoroughly dispirited by this, the giant dropped the spadeful of earth where he stood – and that was the origin of the Wrekin.

The local people of Belgrave in the Midlands of England tell the tale of how their town got its name. Some time after the Norman Conquest, a certain giant named Bel vowed that he would reach Leicester from Mountsorrel in three leaps. He duly mounted his sorrel steed at Mountsorrel and leaped as far as Wanlip (pronounced one-leap of course). Next he landed at Burstall – so called because the impact of his leap was such that rider, horse and saddle literally burst. However, so determined was Bel that he spurred on his half-dead steed and leaped a third time. Rider and horse dropped dead a mere mile and a half short of Leicester and were buried together in Belgrave.

Apart from all the known giant "remains" dotting
the countryside, there is considerable evidence
of giant presence for those observant enough
to find it.

Obviously some knowledge of giant ploys
(such as self-camouflage) is useful to the
would-be tracker.

Some of the larger stone monuments littering
the countryside are believed to be relics in a more
literal sense. For example the Eglone at
Moytirra in Ireland is traditionally thought to
be a giant turned to stone by a magician
following an argument . . .

Certain giants amused themselves by constructing gargantuan roads and castles. One particularly hefty couple, Wade and his spouse Bell, are believed to have built the Mulgrave and Pickering castles and the road running between them. The road was duly dubbed "Wade's causey" or "Wade's wife's causey" because Bell used it when crossing the moors to milk her gigantic cow.

Individually each of these two giants was capable of building a castle singlehandedly but collectively they suffered the handicap of possessing only one hammer between them. This problem they resolved by throwing the hammer to one another after shouting a warning that the tool was on its way.

Little did giants imagine
that insignificant remnants
of their daily existence
would one day be
considered
historical monuments

The following notes give a brief outline of the daily lifestyle of giants including their likes and dislikes, needs and habits.

It should be remembered throughout that giants were normally very solitary individuals who chose to live alone rather than in family units. Indeed, the family entity was a rare phenomenon among the species.

With the exception of occasional giant colonies, there was no developed titan society. This meant there was no specialization of skills to facilitate everyday life. Each individual had to cope to the best of his ability.

GIANT
LIFESTYLE

While in southern climes giants were generally
either naked (to keep cool) or camouflaged
(for shelter and shade), the primeval nordic
titan—like early man—draped himself in the
skins and furs of animals which he had killed for
food. In clothing he sought warmth only—to
his rough epidermis a coarse animal hide felt
like silk.

As time passed and the big men acquired
minimal skills to facilitate their lives, they
learned to fasten together lengths of coarse
cloth.

Warmth comes from animal furs and skins...

Multiple layers act as insulation against the cold.

The giant would tear holes along the edge of the fabric and thread a length of begged, borrowed or stolen cord. Finally he would knot the ends together or loop them around the waist. This tunic style was sometimes ornamented with a ripped hem or the addition of decoration such as a brightly hung clothes line or a wagon wheel. Warmth came from animal fur draped cape-style around the shoulders and giants soon astutely noticed that multiple layers of clothing acted as excellent insulation against unfavorable weather conditions.

In certain habitats giant tribes retained the loin-cloth concept which, for simplicity's sake, could not be matched. Long lengths of cloth could easily be wound around the chubbiest giants and had the advantage of doubling as swaddling clothes for gargantuan offspring.

Predominant colors for giants' clothing have traditionally been dirty greens and russet browns. This factor evidences the race's desire to blend in with the environment for camouflage. Attire reflected mode of life but fashion as we know it played no rôle. As social competition was nonexistent in the giant culture, material needs were confined to essentials. Severity of style thus reflected the basic simplicity of life.

It should be noted that giants are frequently depicted garbed (sometimes scruffily) in Spanish-style Renaissance doublet and hose. We believe this would have been a highly unlikely mode of dress given the lack of expertise of giantesses in the gentle art of dressmaking.

Finally, shoes would seem to have presented a tremendous problem for the giant race. Not only did many giants have poor feet but also their considerable weight would wear out normal leather footwear almost before they had taken a step. Coarse cloth was often wound around the feet in layers with a plank of wood incorporated for each sole. This would be tied with cord and haystacks would be used for padding. There were many other variations on this theme but all were similarly clumsy and uncomfortable. The big race simply had to live with continuous discomfort or alternatively go barefoot and run the risk of stepping on a pair of antlers or a similarly sharp object.

Whereas giants regarded eating more as a necessity for life than as a pleasure, nevertheless they manifested certain preferences. They considered raw meat to be palatable but frequently insisted on aping man by cooking their food.

Few giants bothered with such tasks as baking (which necessitated their "borrowing" sacks of flour from local millers who were seldom happy about this form of acquisition). Culinary expertise was generally limited to boiling. As timing was a total mystery to the giant, the boiling process could easily go on unchecked for days until the contents of the cauldron were reduced to an indistinguishable mush. Fortunately there were few if any gourmets among the big men. Understandably indigestion was common.

The giant's easy-going attitude to life was also reflected in their less than abstemious drinking habits. As man hid his barrels of beer, wine and water for the most part (and after all such barrels were very tiny), giants soon developed their own production methods.

Fortunately slapdash brewing techniques resulted in homemade drinks which were usually a long way from being potent. When by pure chance a batch did turn out to be of any strength, a comparatively small amount would send the giants reeling off to sleep in a happy alcoholic haze before they had time to cause any damage.

Mediterranean titans preferred their own version of wine in the form of a grape-based hooch. This caused considerable dismay among local vineyard owners who would periodically find entire vineyards uprooted overnight. To be fair to the giants, we must add that they would frequently bear a vat or two of their home-made booze as a gift to nearby villages. Unfortunately, as the inhabitants were normally the selfsame vineyard owners who had found their vineyards devastated overnight, the giant offering was often met with something less than enthusiasm.

Closely allied to the giant penchant for drinking was their enjoyment of parties, picnics and other merrymaking. Parties normally took place in the vaulted caves where so many of the big men lived but, as the alcohol offered was not strong and conversations were rather limited intellectually, these were not quite the festive occasions they might have been.

Perhaps this lack of co-ordination in movement is fortunate however.
The combined weight of the "dancers" would otherwise certainly cause devastating chain reactions of landslides, earthquakes and tidal waves.

WORK

Most giants tried to be accepted and liked by small men. Basically they were friendly by nature and loved companionship but they were easily hurt when rejected. The titans would go to considerable lengths to be helpful to smaller men as they could be extremely useful where strenuous or awkward work was required. They could accomplish in an instant what man could labor over for a month.

For their efforts, giant laborers usually received payment in kind. Yet acceptance and friendship among men is what they actively sought and valued the most.

Horns and tusks are useful for digging trenches, ripping up trees, moving logs and so on.

Deforestation and land clearance were activities often entrusted to giant helpers some of whom also boasted pronounced lower molars which were a great asset in uprooting trees.

Giants were also useful city guardians as even
the most gentle of the species was a daunting
sight to a potential invader.

The giant of Carn Galva in Cornwall
(traditionally a giant stronghold since the
invasion mounted by Brutus and Corineus)
was an amiable fellow. He protected the people
of Zennor and Morvah from the giant bandits
of the Lelant Hills, receiving for his pains the
gratitude of the people and probably the odd
sheep or goat.

Fishing was a favorite giant activity but some
of their piscatorial forays were a source of
irritation to fishermen—on numerous occasions
they watched in dismay while giants gathered in
the fishermen's nets and carried off the entire
catch.

Other giants worked happily and
enthusiastically with local fishing fleets. They
would wade out beside the fishermen's boats to
aid in lifting the nets or scoop handfuls of fish
and drop them directly onto the decks.
Occasionally a giant would dam a river in
order to help with freshwater fishing but this
had its risks. Owing to their notoriously bad
memories, they would frequently forget to tear
down the dams and this sometimes caused
flooding.

Obviously
such strenuous
activities,
coupled with
giants' great
height and weight,
led to fatigue
and giants required
frequent rest
periods.
Fortunately insomnia
was uncommon
among the species
and the big men were
capable of
enjoying a
refreshing nap
in most
unusual positions.

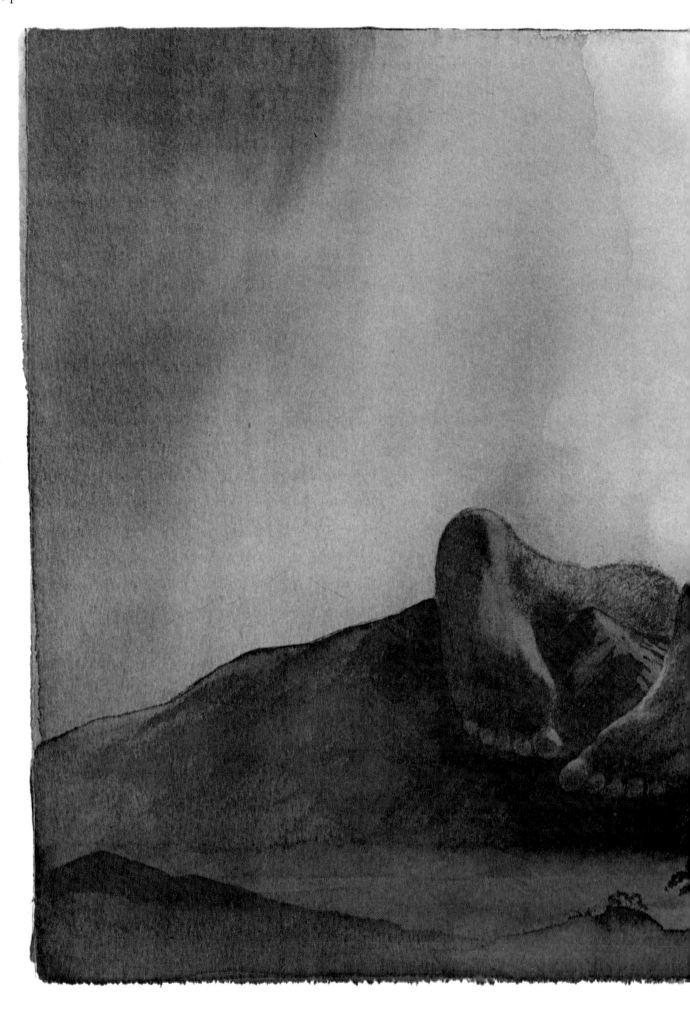

A giant can be much
troubled by low-lying
cloud formations
Should he trip over
some concealed hill
or cliff, he can
cause an interesting
break in the
nebulae

GIANT PASTIMES

As we have seen, pilfering
was a common pastime
among the lazier giants.
An unwary shepherd
could only too easily—
and too late—
notice a huge arm
popping out of a mountain
cave to grab a sheep,
cow or tasty-looking man.

Generally giants did not know how to plough,
cultivate, reap or mill. Nor did they believe in
duplicating the efforts of others. Thus they
were obliged to live on what they could "find".
Among the very few articles which they could
make for themselves successfully were knotted
wooden clubs on which they could lean when
weary.

There were rare examples of giants who
were purely destructive in temperament.

The giants of the Leland Hills were well known
and greatly feared for their destructive natures
as they looted and pillaged and were not averse
to a touch of arson either . . .

In a Danish forest called the Grünewald
on the island of Moën, the strange sight of a
ghostly giant on horseback can sometimes be seen.
This fearsome creature hunts and kills
little forest wood-wives for his sport.

A giant with an even more unusual pastime was
Retho. He specialized in hunting and slaying
kings whom he collected in order to scalp their
chins for their royal beards. Retho was very
keen to add King Arthur's beard to a furry
cloak which he was fashioning with his collection.
Retho politely requested King Arthur to tear
off his own beard and send it to him, promising
that as King Arthur was of such distinguished
lineage, he would sew the king's beard higher
up the cloak than any of the others. Arthur
not unnaturally declined. Determined to get
the beard, Retho challenged the king to single
combat—and lost not only his life but his cloak
and his own beard to boot.

Giants are very proud of their beards
particularly as these can prove an
asset to the big men's lives.
 In winter they provide warmth
(especially when giants are asleep).
Beards also attract various forms of
wildlife. Combing rids the hair
 of parasites and in times of
hardship combing over a cauldron
 can provide a modest meal.

Anything glittery, shiny, tinkly, curiously shaped, edible, drinkable, throwable or indeed interesting in any way at all was coveted by giants. They were practically incapable of walking even a score or so miles before their eyes lit on something that had to be picked up, minutely examined and pocketed. Such magpie-like habits meant that at least some of the giants had acquired large collections. They liked to keep their treasure in great chests which they could open from time to time when they wanted to gloat.

Once a very prosperous giant was travelling home in his native Yorkshire carrying his chest of gold on his back. His journey was long and he was soon so weary that he tripped, swore and dropped his load which sunk into the earth and was buried. This treasure is guarded by a fairy in disguise but its whereabouts remain unknown. The saying goes that finders are keepers just so long as no oaths are uttered by the finder as he drags the chest out of its hiding place.

In the county of Shropshire in England there once lived two giants, believed to be brothers, who had accumulated piles of money which they kept locked up in a big trunk in the dungeons of Stokesay Castle. As is typical with giants, they possessed only one key to the treasure trunk. As the two brothers lived far apart, there was quite a lot of shouting to one another and key throwing when either of the brothers needed to get out any money.

One day the inevitable happened and the giant sending the key over to his brother threw short. The key landed with a plop in the castle moat and there it has stayed until this very day. The treasure is still there in the castle vaults for all we know although treasure seekers say there is a great big black raven perched on the trunk that has no intention of letting anyone break into the chest without the key.

MORE GIANT PASTIMES

In their spare time, giants were keen games players and practical jokers. There was nothing a self-respecting giant would enjoy quite so much as a competitive game. Prestige was all important—the winner won all and a losing giant could be expected to sulk for years, if not in perpetuity.

Many giants (trying to break the record set by the famed giant MacMahon of Ireland no doubt) spent inordinately long periods practicing the hop, step and jump mile (that is to say a mile covered in a single hop, one step and a jump) or striding over houses without touching them (no mean feat on a misty day).

Among giant children graffiti and rock building were popular pastimes. Unfortunately giant offspring occasionally indulged in troublesome and annoying games such as blowing up duststorms, spitting and snowball-rolling. However, as they grew older (luckily), such games generally lost their appeal.

While at certain times in history giants were figures of fun for the human population, many of the big men managed to amuse themselves at our expense too.

A Cornish giant used to stretch out his long arm and snatch a fistful of sailors from a passing ship—much to the consternation both of his victims and of the remaining crew. However, when he had had his fun, the titan would replace his captives unharmed.

In their spare time, giants were keen games players.

Stone-throwing and stone-dropping were very popular pastimes among giants and remnants of these activities are in evidence all over the world. Most are not recognized as being the result of giant games even where a particular type of stone is found miles away from any others of the same sort.

In Orkney one giant was so active that his
memory lingers on in the name given to the
stones littering the islands. These are commonly
called Cubbie Roo Stones after a gigantic
Norse chieftain who lived on the island of Wyre.
To be fair, this noble fellow was not really of
the more featherbrained stone-lobbing variety
of giant and his boulders remain mostly as a
result of his mighty building endeavors
and were dropped either in error or
exasperation . . .

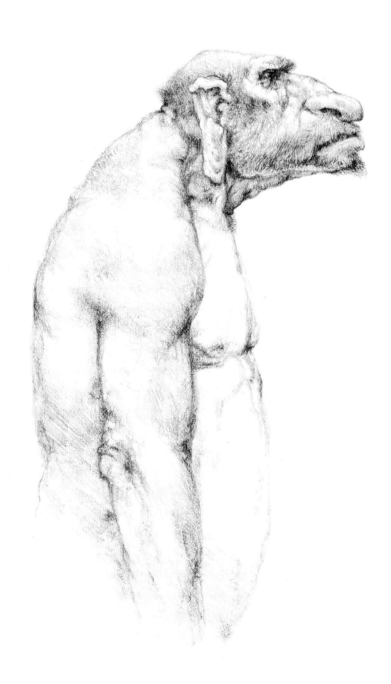

Giants loved to prove themselves in tests of
strength which were used to gauge an
individual's respectability. Rock-carrying was
the most common of these tests and some of the
big men were so practiced in this art that they
developed elongated arms and protruding
chins.

Camouflaged giants could have hours of fun with the unwary. There are few more disconcerting discoveries than to find oneself astride a giant's big toe or kneeling on his upper lip peering up his nose . . .

The mediaeval era offered great potential for fun-loving giants. The curious clothing of the European knight gave the inquisitive titans hours of amusement. Mediaeval man however was *not* amused, and retaliated aggressively. A good sport for the giants was to allow the little men to believe they could emerge victorious from any fray. The small warriors, anxious to prove themselves against the superior size of the giants, would not recognize that they were objects of fun for the big men and would often emerge both with damaged pride and bruised bodies despite the giants' efforts to handle their toy-like opponents carefully.

But it was essentially the clothing adopted by man that amused the giants. A passing knight in shining armor was often just too tempting to be ignored —

— they just had to have a closer look.

Sir Olifaunt, a Chaucerian giant, was one of the
playful titans. He would stop travelling knights
on the road and jestingly challenge them to
combat . . .

At certain times in history it was customary for
warriors to capture fierce giants alive and bring
them home as trophies to be shown off to
family, friends and neighbors. To man's surprise,
many giants taken prisoner after bloody battles
were soon found to be gentle creatures whose
sole desire was to live in harmony with their
fellow men.

Caligorant, famed giant of the Nile, was greatly
feared for his savage habits until he was
captured. Thenceforth he was as docile as a
lamb.

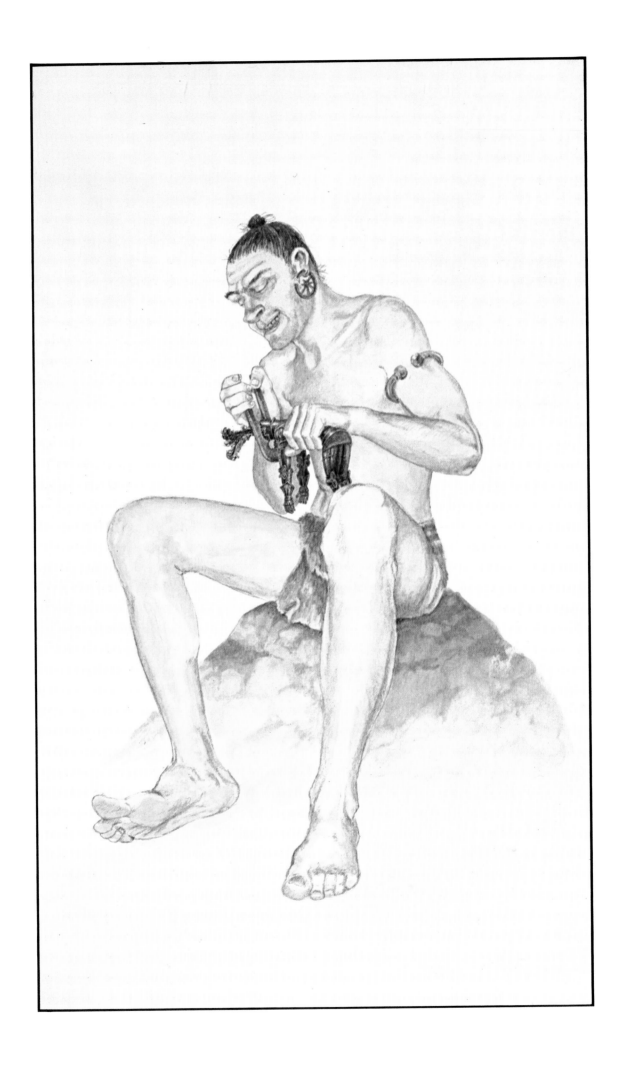

The shiny parts of suits of armor were irresistible attractions to giant men. When knights were not to be found—statues were much appreciated as playthings.

In London Town at the time of King Henry
VIII there lived a giantess called Long Meg of
Westminster. Country-bred Meg decided to
come to London to have some fun, and soon her
exploits were almost as well known and
certainly as popular as those of her king.

Tomboyish Long Meg adored practical jokes
and loved the occasional good fight. However,
she also found time to marry and to run a
successful house of ill-repute in Southwark,
south of the river Thames.

Man tried to play on the inherent inquisitiveness of the giant race. Anti-giant contraptions, such as that shown here, were devised to trap the big men.

This particular device is man-operated. When the curious giant places his eye to the keyhole, the trapper turns the handle, thus releasing the hammer...

Giant children were even more curious.
They were intrigued by the seemingly futile efforts
of man to tap the natural resources of nature.
Farmers toiling with ploughshares were
fascinating sights, as were harvesters, fruit
pickers or haymakers.

The young giants would sometimes decide to
take the objects of their interest home to
play with . . .

GIANTS AS PIONEERS

PECOS BILL

Pecos Bill was a giant back in the days of the Wild West and his memory still lingers on among the cowboys of Texas and New Mexico.

The son of a redoubtable woman (Pecos' mother once slew forty five Indians single-handed), Pecos Bill was believed to be the first of the cowboys.

Mislaid as a child, Pecos was brought up in a pack of coyotes – so successfully, in fact, that to begin with he really believed he was a coyote. Later, when he realized he wasn't, he set out to become as accomplished a Westerner as possible. Soon he was also one of the best cattle-rustlers ever, as he could lasso an entire herd at a time.

Drink had no effect on Bill as he had been weaned on moonshine so he got his kicks from his own inventiveness: as everyone knows, Pecos Bill was not only the inventor of the six-shooter, but also the first train-robber. Nothing daunted Pecos Bill and any rattler or mountain-lion foolish enough to get in his way soon learned the error of its ways. Bill even learned to ride a cyclone and that is no easy feat!

However the giant's efforts at conservation were unfortunately not as successful. When buffaloes were running short, Pecos Bill would skin them alive and then set them free to grow a new hide. This was fine in the summer months but in the winter many of them caught colds and died.

The saddest day in Pecos' life was when he was obliged to shoot his own dear bride, Slue-Foot Sue. What happened was that on their very wedding day, Sue, all decked up in her hooped wedding dress, had a crazy desire to ride Bill's old nag, Widow-Maker. The horse was not so keen on the idea and threw Sue way up into the sky. Well, when Sue eventually hit the ground, the hoops in her dress concertinaed and sent her flying up again. Every time she landed, up she went again. After three whole days and four whole nights of bouncing, poor old Sue was in a sorry state and Pecos Bill, distraught with sorrow, had no option but to shoot his bride to keep her from starving to death.

How Pecos Bill finally met his end is arguable. Some say his search for kicks led him to lace his drink with strychnine, fish hooks and barbed wire, leading to indigestion, loss of appetite and eventual death by starvation when he weighed no more than two tons. Others remember vaguely the visit of a city dude dressed to the nines in shiny ten-gallon hat and well-pressed cowboy outfit. The sight gave Pecos Bill such a kick that he died laughing . . .

PAUL BUNYAN

Another great pioneering spirit was Paul Bunyon. Famed inventor of the lumber trade, Bunyon also possessed a rare intellect. Now we know there were few really great brains among the giants although most of them managed to get along. Paul Bunyon was the exception. The floor of his cave home was littered with papers and books dotted among his hunting gear and blankets. The cave floor was his slate, a charred pine tree his pencil.

This cave Bunyon shared with his moose hound Niagara. This was a fortunate friendship as Niagara did all the hunting when Paul was having a studying bout and the faithful hound would carry home to his master mouthfuls of freshly killed moose, Paul's favorite food.

When Bunyon lost his dog he was understandably distraught. (Niagara had been chasing moose so fast and so far that he collided with the North Pole, crashed through the snow fields and drowned.) Fortunately though his loneliness was shortlived as he rescued and adopted an enormous blue ox calf which he nicknamed Bébé. The animal was gigantic – bright blue and very strong. Soon Paul's superior intellect hit upon a plan. Great things were to be accomplished. Bunyon decided to go south to the new land of opportunity, America. He renamed himself Bunyan, and his baby ox (now no longer such a baby!), Babe.

In the Land of Opportunity Bunyan invented logging – transporting the logs in bundles hung round Babe. Soon the pair attracted the eyes of the world by their labors. Bunyan and Babe were the pioneers of one of the major industries of the world . . .

Some giants were not too happy to hear the wheels
of progress approaching – but they soon found
ways to adapt...

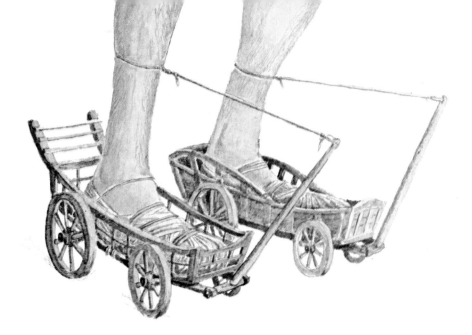

GIANTS ON THE MOVE

While the advent of the wheel certainly
undermined the giants' ambulatory superiority,
the big men soon saw the benefits to be gained
by adapting this invention to their daily needs.

Giants avoid downhill runs
as their momentum is too great.
They have to crouch
in anticipation of loss of control.

Tree trunk
for support
and feeling
the depth
of snow.

GIANTS AND FRIENDSHIP

Alienated by their great size, giants craved companionship and were inordinately grateful for any show of kindness. Sometimes the strangest friendships were struck up, most— but not all—of which were mutually rewarding . . .

A giant and a dwarf once struck up a warm friendship. Having sworn never to part, they set off together to seek adventure. Soon they engaged in combat with a couple of Saracens. These they managed to overcome but not before the dwarf, a courageous little fellow who had cheerfully led the way into battle, had lost an arm.

Next they fought three satyrs. Again the unfortunate dwarf was wounded—this time losing an eye. On a third occasion the dwarf lost a leg. The giant meanwhile had not a scratch on his body. Thrilled at their exploits, he proposed a fourth skirmish . . . but by then the dwarf had learned his lesson and declined.

The giant of Carn Galva was rather playful but this pleasant characteristic had unfortunate results at times. There was one tragic occasion when the giant was playing with a young friend, a villager from Choon. Their game over, the two were taking leave of one another when the giant patted the boy in a friendly way on the head. The boy immediately fell dead at the giant's feet. The big fellow's fingers had gone right though his skull. The giant tried desperately to put the head together again but to no avail. Heartbroken he took the boy in his arms and rocked him to and fro wailing "Oh my son, my son, why didn't they make the shell of thy noddle stronger? A es as plum (soft) as a pie-crust, dough-baked, and made too thin by the half! How shall I ever pass my time without thee to play bob and mop-and-heede? (hide and seek)."

(From William Bottrell's *Hearthside Stories of West Cornwall*)

The poor giant of Carn Galva was never again merry. He pined away and died of a broken heart before seven years had passed.

During one of the unfortunate periods in history
when giants were less than appreciated in many
regions of the world, lived the giant Bolster.
He was another Cornish giant and was of
particularly gigantic dimensions having a stride
of six miles.

At that time, Cornwall was in the grip of a
religious fervor, "Saints" abounded and
could do no wrong in the eyes of
the populace. One such saint was St. Agnes –
a devastatingly beautiful woman but with a
heart of stone where giants were concerned.

Bolster fell head over heels in love with this lady
and even forsook nagging his wife to follow
St. Agnes incessantly. St. Agnes, as we have
already said, was not too partial to giants and
she rejected all Bolster's advances brusquely,
considering it quite unseemly for a married man
to be behaving in such a manner.

One day – being quite exasperated at the giant's
lovelorn countenance, St. Agnes forgot her
normal saintly behavior and played a very cruel
trick on the poor giant. She told Bolster that she
required proof of his love and that he was to fill
a hole in the cliff with his blood. She omitted
however to mention that the hole led into the
sea . . . Lovesick Bolster bled to death.

CYCLOPES

While we have set out to demonstrate as far as possible that the evil giant as he is so often depicted in stories and legends occurs no more frequently than the evil man—although he makes a far more interesting subject for fiction writers—it must be admitted that one specific tribe of giants consisted almost exclusively of unpleasant titans. Here we are of course referring to the Cyclopes or one-eyed giants. Polyphemus is the first of these to spring to mind but curiously there is a wealth of similar tales in many countries of the world indicating that the incidence of one-eyed giants was more widespread than one would have thought and was certainly not restricted to the Mediterranean areas, although they were possibly more prevalent there. We have heard tell of a race of Cyclopean giants called Obigs in Africa who were certainly dangerous although we have no details as to their lifestyle. There were also many solitary living Cyclopes who generally preyed on man. Whether this was due to man's reaction to such repellent-looking creatures is impossible to know.

Closer to home, a giant of this species once lived in a mill at Dalton near Yorkshire and the local people whispered that he made his bread from the flour of ground bones—human bones of course (we rather doubt this as most giants are infinitely clumsy at all things domestic . . .). At all events it seems this giant captured a local boy and decided to keep him as a servant rather than grind him up. In time the boy decided he needed a day off from his labors and asked his master leave to visit the local fair. The giant brusquely refused. The boy, Jack as he was called, resolved not to take "no" for an answer. He waited until the giant dozed off after a heavy meal, seized a hefty kitchen knife and drove it into the giant's one eye. The giant went berserk in his agony and threshed about blindly trying to catch his attacker who could not escape. To hide his identity Jack slew the giant's pet dog, skinned it and donned the skin. Then he escaped, barking madly, between the legs of the Cyclops.

Another rather repulsive Cyclops plagued the area around Sessay in the North Riding area of Yorkshire. His big appetite led him to pay daily visits to nearby homesteads to acquire the necessary food for Cyclopean sustenance.

At this same time a young man, Guy, son of Sir John D'Aunay, sought the hand of a local damsel named Joan Darell. Now Joan, it seems, was in no particular hurry to get married for she demanded of the young man the head of the gluttonous Cyclops as a condition of their betrothal.

No sooner had the young man agreed than the giant was seen stalking out of a nearby wood bent on collecting a sack of flour from the village mill. As the young Guy dutifully buckled on his sword the wind changed causing the sails of the mill to turn. One of these sails struck the giant squarely on his head. He fell to the ground stunned and stalwart Sir Guy rushed up to him and drove his sword through the monster's eye.

A GULLIVER WORLD

As we have seen, Man and the giants shared the same earthly environment and, in most cases, the giants' stature was accentuated further by the far smaller proportionate size of the landscape and the surrounding flora and fauna. But there was also a giant land. Well off the beaten track, with little possibility of incursions by hostile men, the contours of the land itself and the fruits of Nature were proportionately grandiose.

We know there exist areas where flora and fauna have developed to often spectacular dimensions due to such phenomena as exaggerated temperature and humidity. In these regions too giant men predominated. The great quantity of carbon dioxide exhaled by a colony of giants logically led to proportionately greater growth in the surrounding plant life which in turn produced the greater amount of oxygen required by giant men. The laws of adaptation work both ways . . .

In Brobdingnag, the land of giants visited by Lemuel Gulliver in his travels and described by Jonathan Swift in his book *Gulliver's Travels*, corn grew forty feet in height, hedges one hundred and twenty and trees were "so lofty that I could make no computation of their altitude." Voices were greatly magnified—"at first I certainly thought it was thunder" while even a gentle breeze seemed a gale.

Lemuel Gulliver became something of a celebrity in Brobdingnag and, indeed, he was shown off throughout the land in much the same way giants were exhibited in Europe at the same period. Eventually he was taken into the royal household. Obviously however his tiny stature had its disadvantages in such huge surroundings. Flies, bees or even a sneeze became far more than irritating and, as for small mammals—their dimensions, odors and habits became well-nigh dangerous.

Gulliver was at one point presented with a
sailing boat for his pleasure and this he would
row or sail in a trough provided for this purpose,
a "wind" when necessary being whipped up
by the ladies of the court with their fans or by
the pages with their breath. It was while thus
employed one day that Gulliver nearly met an
untimely end. A frog had got into the trough
unperceived and this creature climbed up onto
Gulliver's boat, almost overturning it . . .
Gulliver managed to get it out but not before it
had daubed his face and clothes "with its
odious slime."

On another occasion a monkey grabbed
Gulliver and, imagining him to be one of its
offspring, fondly attempted to force feed the
unfortunate prisoner . . .

Seated on the king's table in front of one of the
salt cellars, Gulliver was plagued by flies "and
these odious insects, each of them as big as a
Dunstable lark, hardly gave me any rest while
I sat at dinner . . . Sometimes they would fix
upon my nose or forehead where they stung me
to the quick, smelling very offensively, and I
could easily trace that viscous matter, which
our naturalists tell us enables those creatures
to walk with their feet upwards upon a ceiling."

The Selfish Giant

There was once a giant's garden where the sun always shone, beautiful birds sang and magnificent trees grew. Exotic flowers bloomed and delicious scents were carried on the balmy breeze.

The owner of this delightful spot had gone for a short visit (seven years) to his friend the ogre in Cornwall. During his absence, local children – their young senses revelling in the loveliness around them – had fallen into the habit of considering this paradise to be theirs. For hours they would play there, stopping only when it was time for them to go home to bed.

When the seven year visit was over, the giants had nothing more to say to each other so the garden's owner returned. Being a very selfish giant, he was not pleased when he saw so many happy little children playing in his garden. He shooed them away angrily, built a huge wall around his garden and threatened to prosecute all "tresspersers".

Mother Nature was not happy with this state of affairs. When spring came to the land, the giant's property was excluded. Elsewhere trees burst into bud, flowers peeked up from the grass and the sun softly shone but the giant's garden remained locked in winter. The trees were covered with snow, the air was frostbitten and the north wind howled.

The giant could not understand why spring was so late in coming. Every day he would awaken, gaze sadly out of his window and remember wistfully how enchanting his garden used to be. Now one day when he looked out the giant noticed a strange sight. Some small children had crept through a hole in his wall. They had clambered up some of his trees and the branches on which they were perched had burst into blossom. Indeed the sun was trying to shine. In one corner of the garden however winter had not slackened its grip. At the bottom of a snow-clad tree stood a little boy, crying pitifully as he looked up into the branches above him.

The tree was trying to coax him to
climb up, stretching down its branches towards
him but he could not reach them. This sight
softened the giant's heart and he opened his
door to go to the child's aid. But, as he appeared,
the other children fled and the garden again
became wintry and sad. In his misery the little
boy had not noticed the giant. The big man
crept up behind him, picked him up and sat
him on a branch of the tree.

Immediately the tree burst into bloom. The child in his joy embraced the giant. Seeing there was nothing to fear, the other children came tripping back into the garden and with them came the spring . . .

Note: Giants are notoriously bad spellers.

Years went by. Each day groups of children would come to see the giant who by now was too old to play — he simply sat happily and watched their games.

But one day when the children
came into the garden to play they
found the old giant lying dead,
covered with a blanket of flowers...

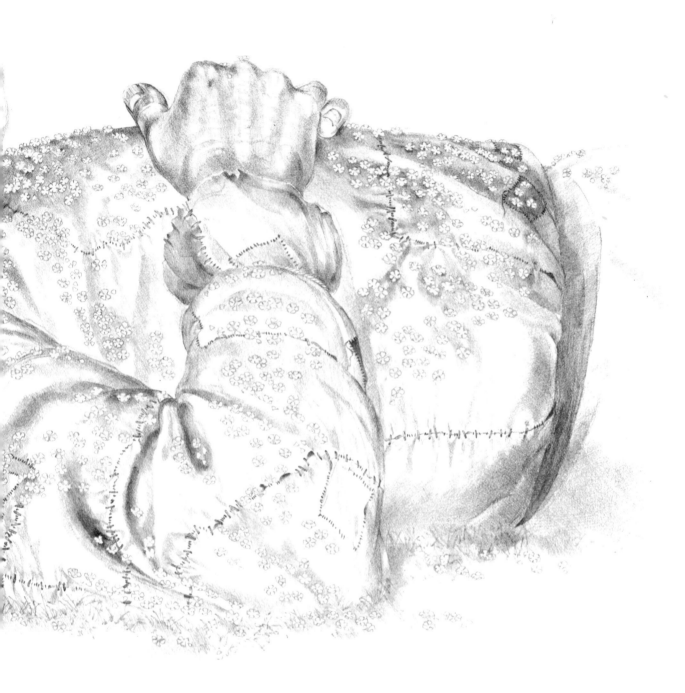

Adapted from Oscar Wilde's story *The Selfish Giant*.

Located off the west coast of Scotland are the Shetlands—peaceful islands today although it was not always so. As we have already mentioned, in the eighth and ninth centuries the Norwegians came to the Orkneys and Shetlands, bringing with them both their giants and their trolls (or trows as the Scots renamed them). As time went by the giants slowly disappeared whereas the trows diminished in size and adapted to their new environment quite happily. However they retained all the annoying little habits learned and practiced in their former homeland.

One giant who still remained in the Kaems hills of Shetland was plagued to distraction by these tiresome trows. They would clamber all over him, exploring his nose and ears, pulling his hair and generally making a nuisance of themselves.

One day the giant decided he could stand it no longer. He devised a plan to capture all the trows in a huge creel. This he intended to carry over to Norway where he could deposit the little pests before returning to Shetland. The

giant was well pleased with his idea and began to make an enormous creel out of straw. When he had finished he took this to a spot where the trows habitually congregated on moonlit nights. As soon as they made their appearance, he scooped them up and dropped them into the creel, pulling its cord tight to prevent his little prisoners from escaping.

Unfortunately, the creel was so large that the giant could not lift it. He decided it would be easier to drag it to a nearby hilltop so that he could stand at the bottom of the hill and hoist the creel over his shoulder. The ground was rocky and uneven. Sharp stones tore at the bottom of the creel, weakening it to such an extent that when the giant finally raised it, its base fell out, liberating all the captive trows.

No one is quite certain of the fate of the poor giant but it is believed that he went back to Norway for a little peace and quiet.

An arch-enemy of the giant race was young Cornish Jack who set out to win fame and fortune with his exploits of pitting his wits against the most dangerous of giants.

Jack's first goal was to rid his native Cornwall of the giant Cormoran of St. Michael's Mount, an evil-tempered cattle-rustler. This Cormoran had plagued local farmers for years and Jack resolved to take drastic action.

One dark night, Jack dug a deep pit on the Mount in front of Cormoran's castle. This he concealed with sticks, straw and earth. In the morning, Jack blew a mighty blast on his horn. The giant awoke with a start. Understandably irritated at this rude interruption, the titan rushed out of his castle towards Jack, threatening him with all manner of unpleasant punishments. Suddenly he found himself tumbling headfirst into Jack's trap. Now the boot was firmly on the other foot. Jack first taunted his adversary, then raised his pickaxe and let it fall with a thud on the giant's head, killing him on the spot.

Soon the news of Jack's daring had spread all over the land and he was awarded the official title of Jack The Giant Killer and presented with a decorated sword and belt in recognition of his services. However this is not the end of our tale...

Some time later, Jack was travelling towards Wales when he felt a great weariness come over him. He sat down to rest awhile and soon fell into a deep slumber. A certain giant named Blunderbore came upon the sleeping Jack and recognized his identity. Having sworn revenge for the slaying of the giant Cormoran, he picked up the boy and bore him off towards his bone-strewn castle.

Jack awoke at this point and was quite alarmed to find himself draped across the shoulder of a mighty giant. The lad was doubly dismayed when he saw the human bones which littered the huge chamber of the castle in which he was imprisoned.

Now Blunderbore had a brother who lived nearby. Having decided it would be a pleasant notion if he and his kin were to dine together on tender Jack, Blunderbore set off to invite him. Meanwhile Jack surveyed his prison and noticed some strong cords in a corner. These the lad knotted to form two nooses and, when he saw the giants returning, he positioned himself by a slit in the castle wall. When the giants drew close, Jack quickly dropped a noose over each of their heads, pulled the cords tight over a hefty beam and tugged as hard as he could. As soon as the giants were quite blue in the face, Jack slid down one of the cords and slew them with his sword.

At one point in his travels Jack teamed up in his exploits with King Arthur's only son. Having fallen on hard times due to their unfailing generosity, the young pair were seeking food and shelter when they came across the home of Jack's own uncle who himself just happened to be a large giant. Now Jack simply desired rest and nourishment and he wished his uncle no harm. Unfortunately his kinsman was reputed to be rather mean and fierce. So Jack went up to the castle alone and tricked him by

pretending that his friend, the young prince, was in his wake with an army of one thousand men bent on slaying the giant. Well, Jack's uncle was really not quite as fierce as he made out. Indeed he flew into a panic and made plans to hide himself in the depths of his castle dungeons, begging Jack to lock the heavy cellar doors behind him until the "invaders" had left. This Jack gladly did and while his poor uncle lay quaking down in the cellar, Jack and the young prince made merry feasting.

On the morrow, Jack released the giant explaining that the armies had withdrawn. His giant uncle in his gratitude gave Jack a magic sword, a cap of knowledge, shoes of speed and a cloak that made the wearer invisible – gifts that proved valuable to the boy . . .

Some time later Jack decided for king and country to challenge a huge goggle-eyed giant and his horrible brother. But the giants were no match for Jack's magic. The boy easily slew the first creature and then dealt with his fearsome brother. Cutting off the dead titans' heads, he sent them to the court of King Arthur.

This terrible pair had kept many prisoners behind bars in their cave home. From time to time they would select a plump victim for a special repast. Jack soon freed these unfortunate prisoners and they all went to a neighboring castle where they made merry with feasting and revelry.

In the midst of this rejoicing there entered a messenger as pale as death. He warned the assembly of the approach of the giant Thundell,

a terrible two-headed monster who had sworn revenge on Jack for the death of his two kinsmen, the goggle-eyed giant and his brother. Jack was unperturbed. The castle in which they were had a moat around it and a single drawbridge permitted entry. Jack arranged that the bridge be sawn nearly through on both sides near the middle. Soon the giant could be seen approaching, muttering terrible threats. The earth shook under his feet. But Jack put on his shoes of swiftness, crossed the drawbridge and paraded himself in front of the enemy as a taunt. The giant followed Jack who led him round and round the castle. Then the boy quickly crossed the bridge. The giant followed wielding his mighty club but, when he reached the middle, the bridge could no longer bear the weight of his huge bulk and it broke, sending the giant headfirst into the moat beneath.

Jack laughed and jeered as the giant struggled to get out of the moat. A cart rope was brought and this Jack looped and dropped over the giant's two heads. A team of horses dragged the giant to the edge of the moat where Jack struck off his heads.

Soon the famed Jack was off on his travels again
to seek new adventures. After passing through
many counties, he came across a solitary
cottage at the foot of a particularly awesome
mountain. A very old man lived in this house
and he gladly invited Jack in. When he
recognized Jack as the famed giant killer, he
told him that at the very top of the mountain
near his cottage was an enchanted castle in
which lived a fearsome giant called
Galligantus and his companion, a wicked
conjuror. This infamous couple had lured many
knights and ladies into their castle and had then
transformed them by magic into a variety of
shapes. The most grieved of their victims was a
duke's daughter. Kidnapped from her father's
garden, she had been borne away to the castle
in a chariot harnessed to two fire-belching
dragons. There she was changed into a hind.

The old man told Jack that countless brave
knights had attempted to storm the castle and
rescue its prisoners but most had been killed by
the two savage griffins that guarded the castle
gates. Jack however had his magic cloak and
so would be able to enter in safety. So Jack set
off. Putting on his cloak, he climbed to the top
of the mountain. He passed the two fearsome
griffins unperceived and saw a trumpet hanging
on the castle gate under which was written
"Whoever doth this Trumpet blow,
   Shall cause the Giant's overthrow!"

Jack took the trumpet and blew a mighty blast.
The castle gates flew open revealing the giant
and the magician rooted to the spot in fear.
Jack swiftly disposed of the giant, the magician
was swept away in a whirlwind and all the
captured knights and ladies resumed their
human shapes. Finally the enchanted castle
vanished forever.

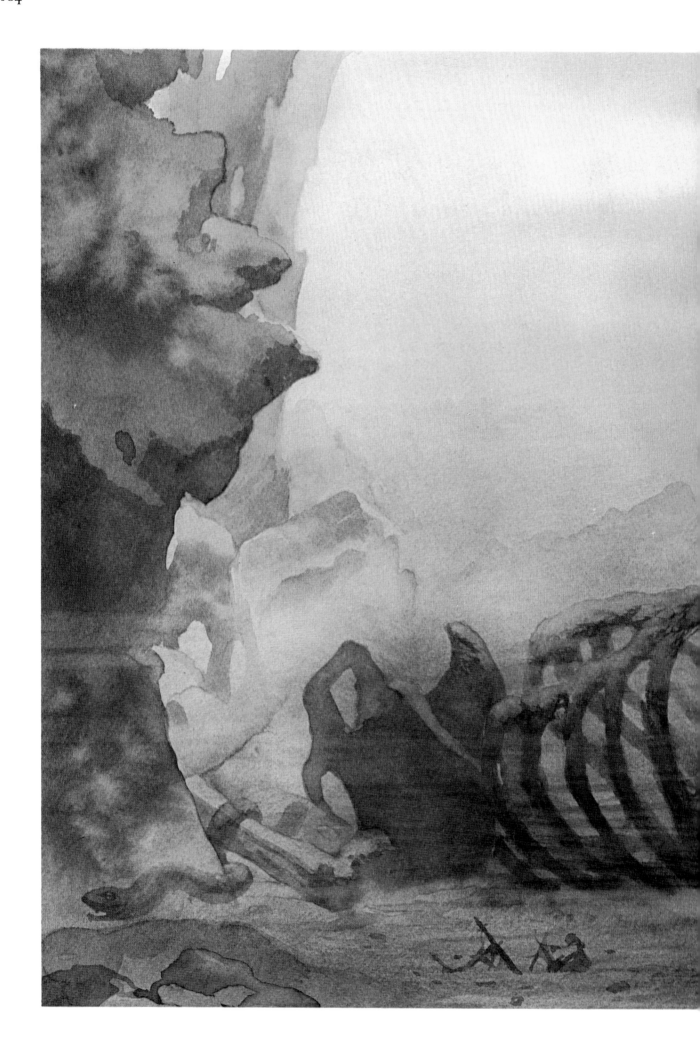

AN ENDANGERED
SPECIES

That the giant is nearing
extinction as a species is,
we think, indisputable.

Man's basic distrust of all that is alien to him,
his habitual defensiveness, tendency towards
jealousy, preoccupation with appearance and
propensity for aggression are root causes in the
near extinction of the giant race. We have
already seen that the giant's physique is largely

redundant to survival in these modern days,
yet there is no doubt in our minds that, given a
little compassion, understanding and
imagination, there is no reason whatsoever why
the remaining giants should not live a happily
integrated life in today's society.

Although sightings continue
(notably of snow giants and
particularly in the Indo-Chinese mountains,
Central China and Eastern Tibet) they are
becoming very rare indeed in Europe and, in the
Americas, even the once prolific Sasquatch
vegetarian giants are now only rarely seen in the
mountains of British Columbia. Is this
an artificial ''extinction'' caused by giants

preferring to hide themselves away in safety,
only showing themselves when natural
conditions make it essential for them to draw
nearer to human habitations in order to forage
for food, or is this a logical disparition
of a race that has been hunted unmercifully for
centuries? We do know that the adults
of the species have developed a marked
tendency to lead a solitary life. The species is
traditionally male-oriented but whether this
is a natural phenomenon resulting from the
birth of more male than female babies, or
whether this is due to a chauvinistic disregard of
marital life is difficult to ascertain.

Hopefully something will be done to prevent the
complete extinction of the giant race.

The giant is, after all,
inextricably a part of our lives—we
only have to look at the traces of his presence
that lie all around us . . .

BIBLIOGRAPHY

Encyclopedia of World Mythology,
Octopus Books Limited, London 1975.

New Larousse Encyclopedia of Mythology,
Hamlyn, London – First pub. 1959.

Funk & Wagnalls Standard Dictionary of Folklore, Mythology and Legend,
New English Library, London 1972.

Reader's Digest Folklore, Myths and Legends of Britain,
Hodder and Stoughton, London 1973.

Ellis Davidson, H.R., *Gods and Myths of Northern Europe*,
Penguin Books Ltd, London 1964.

Magnusson, Magnus, *Hammer of the North*,
Orbis Publishing, London 1976.

Robinson, H.S. & Wilson, K.,
The Encyclopedia of Myths & Legends of All Nations,
Doubleday and Company Inc, New York 1950.

Bord, Janet & Colin, *Mysterious Britain*,
The Garnstone Press Ltd, London 1972.

Chatwin, Bruce, *In Patagonia*,
Jonathan Cape, London 1977.

Frazer, Sir James George, O.M., F.R.S., F.B.A., *The Golden Bough*,
Macmillan and Company, London 1906.

Grinnell, George Bird, *Pawnee Hero Stories and Folk-Tales*,
David Nutt, London 1893.

Lee, Polly Jae, *Giant – The Pictorial History of the Human Colossus*,
A.S. Barnes & Co Inc, New Jersey 1970.

Rees, Alwyn & Brinley, *Celtic Heritage*,
Thames & Hudson, London 1961.

Vitaliano, Dorothy B., *Legends of the Earth*,
Indiana University Press, 1973.

Wendt, H. *I Looked for Adam*,
Weidenfeld & Nicolson, London 1955.

Wilson, Colin, *Mysteries*,
Hodder and Stoughton, London 1978.

Wood, E.J., *Giants and Dwarfs*,
R. Bentley, 1868.

Ariosto, Ludovico, *Orlando Furioso*
(Translated by Guido Waldman),
Oxford University Press, London 1974.

Bottrell, William, *Traditions and Hearthside Stories of West Cornwall*,
W. Cornish, Penzance 1870.

Briggs, K.M., *The Fairies in Tradition and Literature*,
Routledge & Kegan Paul Ltd, London 1967.

Briggs, K.M., *A Dictionary of British Folk-Tales*,
Routledge & Kegan Paul Ltd, London 1971.

Briggs, K.M. and Tongue, R.L., *Folktales of England*,
Routledge & Kegan Paul Ltd, London 1965.

Croker, T. Crofton Esq,
Fairy Legends and Traditions of the South of Ireland,
Swann Sonnenschein & Co, 1862.

Fairholt, F.W., F.S.A., *Gog and Magog*,
John Camden Hotten, London 1859.

Foster Forbes, J., F.R.A.I., F.S.A. Scot., *Giants of Britain*,
Thomas Publications Ltd, Birmingham 1945.

Henderson, William,
Notes on the Folk-Lore of the Northern Counties of England and the Borders,
Published for the Folklore Society by W. Satchell,
Peyton & Co, London 1879.

Jacobs, Joseph, *English Fairy Tales*,
David Nutt, London 1890.

Jones-Baker, Doris, *The Folklore of Hertfordshire*,
B.T. Batsford Ltd, London 1977.

Lofthouse, Jessica, *North-Country Folklore*,
Robert Hale, London 1976.

Manning-Sanders, Ruth, *A Book of Giants*,
Methuen & Co Ltd, London 1962.

A Book of Giants
Selected by William Mayne, Hamish Hamilton, London 1968.

Porteous, Alexander, *Forest Folklore, Mythology, and Romance*,
George Allen & Unwin Ltd, London 1928.

Puttenham, George, *The Arte of English Poesie*
(1589), A. Constable and Co, London 1895.

Walton, Evangeline, *The Children of Llyr*,
Ballantine Books, New York 1971.

The Story of Jack and the Giants,
Cundall & Addey, London 1851.

Burne, Charlotte Sophia, *Shropshire Folk-Lore*
(from the collections of Georgina F. Jackson),
Routledge & Kegan Paul Ltd (Trübner & Co), London 1883.

A Treasury of American Folklore,
edited by B. A. Botkin, Crown Publishers Inc, New York 1944.